# Amazing Chenilled
# Quilted
# Photography

## Exploring Fabric, Color & 4 Teriffic Textured Techniques!

## Tammie Bowser

Bowser Publications / Mosaic Quilt Studio    South Pasadena, California

# Amazing Chenilled
# Quilted Photography

Exploring Fabric, Color & 4 Teriffic Textured Techniques!

## Tammie Bowser

Copyright © 2006 by Tammie Bowser
First Printing January 2006

Editors: Sharon Hayes
Photography: Tammie Bowser
Book Design & Illustrations: Tammie Bowser

All quilts designed and made by Tammie Bowser except where indicated.

Attention Teachers:
Bowser Publications encourages you to use this book as a text for teaching. Contact us at www.QuiltedPhoto.com or at 626-799-5998 for more information about our teacher support program.

Library of Congress Cataloging in Publication Data
Bowser, Tammie
      Simply amazing quilted photography / Tammie Bowser
      ISBN 1-887467-66-1  (paper trade)
      1. Quilting. 2. Quilting--Art.
      3. Art.
      I. Title.

Published by:
      Mosaic Quilt Studio
      917 Fremont, PMB138
      South Pasadena, California 91030

Printed in the U.S.A.

# Table Of Contents

- ◆ Creativity
- ◆ What is Quilted Photography?
- ◆ Why use Texture?
- ◆ What happens when you use texture and Quilted Photography together?

- ◆ What is the difference between color and value?
- ◆ Four ways to choose the colors for your quilt
- ◆ The 8-8-8 rule
- ◆ How to sort your fabrics by value
- ◆ Value is the key!
- ◆ How to choose a great photograph
- ◆ How to take better photos

- ◆ Rules for choosing fabrics to create texture
- ◆ About the fabrics
- ◆ How to prepare and organize fabrics
- ◆ Fabric Cutting Tips
- ◆ Size and scale
- ◆ How to read the patterns
- ◆ Grid Guides and how to use them
- ◆ About the stabilizers

- ◆ What is this technique?
- ◆ Fabrics suitable for technique
- ◆ Preparation Instructions
- ◆ Putting it together
- ◆ Stencils
- ◆ Possible Variations
- ◆ Examples

- ◆ What is this technique?
- ◆ Fabrics suitable for technique
- ◆ Preparation Instructions
- ◆ Putting it together
- ◆ Possible Variations
- ◆ Examples
- ◆ Sample Pattern

# Table Of Contents

# Acknowledgement

Thank you to Angela, for being my perfect little girl. When God made you, he picked you out of all the angels in heaven just for me. You are the reason I work hard. I love you.

Thank you Sandra, for being willing to help me whenever and however I need it! It would have been impossible to work the way I did in 2005 with out you! I love you too!

Thank you Lord for the true, fountain of creativity you have given me. I promise I will keep sharing all of the creative ideas with anyone who is willing to listen!

# Preface

When the first book "Simply Amazing Quilted Photography" was written, I had no idea that any other books would come after it! To my great surprise, one and a half years later the book "More Amazing Quilted Photography" came along!

Before I get started with the third book in this series of "Quilted Photography" books, I want to give you an idea about what you will find, and how it is different from the first two books. First of all we will explore texture. This book is all about texture. In the other two books the fabrics were flat, but in this book I show you how to raise the photograph off the surface of the quilt in amazingly simple ways. I'll also introduce you to some new types of fabrics.

In the last two books, we made a lot of portraits of people. I have some people in this book also, but I wanted to introduce some other abstract images and flowers. I did this so you can get more ideas about what is possible with "Quilted Photography". The patterns for these images are included in the book and I have made the images available to you on my website.

The book also contains some familiar topics because the basic ideas of "Quilted Photography" will always remain the same like: color value, fabric organization, choosing photographs, how to use software etc. Even though the topics are the same, please read them again in this book because I have added some updates that apply to the techniques in previous books and also to the new ideas in this book. These are the most important concepts for Quilted Photography and in some instances the new ideas will make all of your photo quilt projects simpler and easier.

Finally, I have a new newsletter that you can't miss! You won't have to wait two years for more ideas, you will get new ideas every month. So, if you want to make fantastic landscapes, still life or portriates of people, then look to my conclusion to learn how to get your email newsletter subscription!

# Introduction to Quilted Photography with Texture

## In this chapter

◆ Creativity
◆ What is Quilted Photography?
◆ Why use Texture?
◆ What happens when you use texture and Quilted Photography together?

## Creavitity

Creative ideas, for me, always seem to begin with a question. I may see something that I like. It could be a rug, a painting or the fluffy leaves on a tree. It really could be anything.

In this book we are creating texture. I first thought about applying texture to quilts while admiring a painting. The painting was not flat on the surface of the canvas; it had amazing texture that made me see movement, and depth. I started wondering if it were possible to create this kind of texture with fabric. This is how my exploration began. I already knew that I could make a photograph with fabric, however I didn't know if the photographic picture would be visible, or disappear when I add texture.

## What Is Quilted Photography?

While studying graphic design, and computers I discovered that computerized photographs are not really photographs at all, they are just small squares of color that are arranged in a way that causes you to see an image. The more squares that are used to create the image, the clearer the image appears.

This concept works for fabric, tile or anything you can think of. It also works if the squares of color are dots, stars, triangles or any other shape. If you want to test this theory just find any book, newspaper or magazine, and examine a photograph with a magnifying glass. You will see small dots of color.

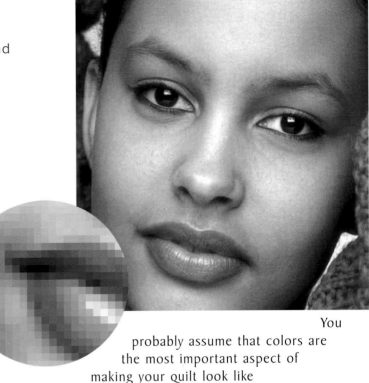

You probably assume that colors are the most important aspect of making your quilt look like a real photograph. Well that assumption is wrong! Value is the key! How is it possible to use colors like blue, and purple and orange for a face? The colors are so unrealistic, yet the photograph is so real. Well that is because color value is much more important than just color alone. Color value is how light or dark a color is in relation to the other fabrics surrounding it. In chapter 2, I will show you how to sort your fabrics by color value. This special process will enable you to make a black and white image using colored fabrics!

Humans can see millions of colors, and most of the printed photographs you see in books, and magazines have hundreds of colors and shades in them. It would be a nightmare to manage a quilting project that has hundreds of different fabrics!

I have experimented with different numbers of fabrics. The maximum number of fabrics that I have found to be manageable is 24. This number of fabrics will make your Quilted Photo projects beautiful, and intriguing! Over the last few years since the first book, I have continued to experiment with the numbers of fabrics and have found that you can use as few as 8 and still get a fabulous photographic image! For the quilts in this book I have used only eight to twelve fabrics for each project to prove this theory.

## Why Use Texture?

The simple reason is, the ability to apply texture will give you more ways to be creative. I enjoy all of the Quilted Photography techniques but each technique has a different look. The textured quilts in this book have their own looks as well and I like to choose textured techniques for images such as animals and abstracts. The textured photo quilts look different than all other photo quilts because the images are softend and abstracted ...... but the picture is there!

The texture is great because you can use fewer fabrics. The edges of the fabrics blend together to make softer edges and appear to be more fabrics then you really have.

All of the technique has several layers of stacked fabrics. With some techniques, the background fabric peeks out and becomes a wonderful surprise element of your quilt design.

## What happens when you use texture and Quilted Photography together?

The first textured quilt I made was a faux chenilled technique you will learn in chapter 4. It is the kitty quilt on the front cover of this book. For this technique you have to first make an image, following a pattern, then slash the picture with a rotary cutter! "Oh my goodness!", I felt panic the first time I cut up my quilt! But, when it was done, I was surprised because it worked! And I liked it! I was excited and began wondering, what else is possible? In chapters 4 - 7 you will learn all of the textured techniques I have discovered.

# Understanding Color, Value & Photographs

## In this chapter

◆ What is the difference between color and value?
◆ Four ways to choose the colors for your quilt
◆ The 8-8-8 rule
◆ How to sort your fabrics by value
◆ Value is the key!
◆ How to choose a great photograph
◆ How to take better photos

This chapter is about understanding the basic elements of Quilted Photography. Read this chapter carefully because really understanding these concepts can be the difference between making a stunning quilt or an average quilt.

## What Is The Difference Between Color And Value?

Another word for color is hue. A example of a hue is red, blue, green etc. Value is how light or dark a fabric is in relation to the other fabrics in your color palette. In the example below, the green swatch and the gray swatch both have the same value but the green swatch also has a green hue. If you look at these two swatches through our blue valuation filter, you will absolutely see that the values are the same.

A color palette is the collection of fabrics used to make your quilt. The most important step in making a photo quilt is arranging your fabrics in order (from light to dark) by value. If you understand value you have the most important element of Quilted Photography under control. Keep reading to learn how to arrange your fabrics in order by value.

## Four Ways To Choose The Colors For Your Quilt

A color palette is a collection of fabrics chosen for a quilted photo project. Choosing the colors for your quilted image is the most creative part of the whole process! Your quilted photograph will become art with your selection of colors.

While shopping for your fabric, you may choose any colors you like but your choices will determine the final look of your quilted photo. For example your quilt will have a sophisticated look if you choose muted colors or neutral shades as your color palette. If you select primary colors, or very bright colors, your quilt will have a lively, fun look.

A very important rule to keep in mind while choosing your colors is to stay in one color intensity. For example, if you have muted shades, choose muted shades for all of your fabrics. Or if you choose bright shades, then choose all bright shades because a fabric that is of the opposite intensity will stand out unattractively. There are several types of color palettes you can try for choosing your colors I will explain each of them.

Restricted color palette
A restricted color palette is a very restricted range of color. This range can have as few as 2 colors. For example you can use a range from dark purple to light pink as shown in this example.

Random color palette
A random color palette is made up of fabrics of any color combination. Choosing your color palette at random is fun! I call a quilted photo made with a random color palette the ultimate scrap quilt! The random color palette is the

most surprising type of palette. It really is hard to believe that putting a collection of totally unrelated fabrics together will create a beautiful photographic quilt. You can even use all of your favorite fabrics. Once you make a photo quilt with a random color palette, you will understand the importance of color value once and for all. You will not have to make any hard color decisions; you will only have to remember to get light, medium, and dark fabrics. This example has lots of colors that are unrelated, but they are arranged in order by value. The best way to see the values of a random collection of fabrics is to use the photocopy method to sort the fabrics.

**Single color palette**
A single color palette is made up of just one color starting with the lightest, all the way to the darkest shades of the hue. This type of palette will work well with any image. It will be like making a colorized black and white photo.

**Realistic color palette**
A realistic color palette is made of fabric that closely resemble the colors of the original photograph. Choosing the fabrics for a realistic color palette is the most challenging type of palette to put together. It is more challenging because you will have to consider the colors and values of the fabrics at the same time. This could mean you will have to shop around to find just the right fabrics to match the color and values.

To make your own patterns with realistic colors, you will need to upgrade to one of the paid version of "Quilted Photo" softwares. I

don't suggest you try a realistic color palette for your first project.

Choosing fabric seems to be the hardest part of the "Quilted Photography" project for my students. I know it can get confusing when you are in the middle of a quilting store surrounded by 1000's of fabric bolts! I have been thinking about this problem for a while and I have come up with two surprisingly easy shortcuts that make choosing fabric less of a dilemma.

To use the first shortcut, start by choosing one fabric. Use the colors in the first fabric as a clue for choosing the next fabric. Keep choosing your fabrics, starting with the light value. Let the last fabric you have chosen be a clue for the next and your palette will have a wonderful, smooth transition from one fabric to the next.

For the second shortcut, go to the thread section of your quilt store. Look at the beautiful variegated threads. You should see a beautiful assortment of cottons, rayons, polyesters and even metallic. They all can be a starting point for choosing your colors. You can use more than one type of thread, for example pick one dark and one light spool to use together on one project. Variegated threads have fantastic color combination that are already worked out for you, and as an added bonus, the thread will be perfect for stitching your project later!

## The 8-8-8 Rule

Another helpful guideline I use when choosing my fabrics is what I call the 8-8-8 Rule. In the first book, I used 24 fabrics for each quilt and I wanted my students to be sure to have an even number of light, medium and dark fabrics. I divided the 24 fabrics into three even parts to determine that it is necessary to have 8 light valued fabrics, 8 medium valued fabrics, and 8 dark valued fabrics. If you decide to use fewer fabrics, the rule is the same. The difference is the total number of fabrics, your total number must be divided by three. For

Photocopied fabrics sorted by color value

| 15 | 18 | 17 | 13 | 19 | 21 | 22 | 14 | 23 |

example, if you have 9 fabrics, you would have 3 light, 3 medium, and 3 dark fabrics. For this book we will still call it the 8-8-8 rule, but now you know this means you must have an even amount of light, medium, and dark fabrics and the total number of fabrics is your choice.

Your goal is to have colored fabrics that represent shades from white to black. Don't be afraid to pick really light shades, as well as really dark shades because they are all necessary. You should be able to easily follow the 8-8-8 Rule while choosing your fabrics.

Do not worry about putting the fabrics in the exact order by color value yet, you'll be able to do that later, just concentrate on the 8-8-8 Rule while shopping.

## How To Sort Your Fabrics By Value

I have found that it is hard for me to see the color value of fabrics with my naked eye. My eyes are easily fooled by the colors. To solve this problem, I use two processes that allow me to see the values of the fabrics separately from the colors.

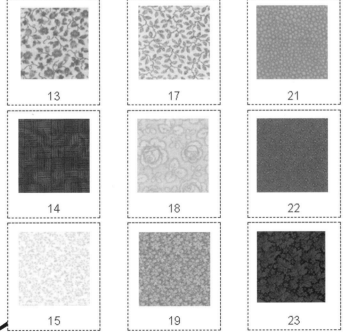

| 13 | 17 | 21 |
| 14 | 18 | 22 |
| 15 | 19 | 23 |

Cut out the photocopies of the numbered swatches

### Method 1

Cut a small piece of each fabric you will be using to make your photo quilt. Photocopy the forms at the end of this chapter, tape one fabric piece in each of the boxes. Make a black and white photocopy of the forms. IMPORTANT: The copy machine must capture grayscale. The photocopy will erase the colors, and only show you the value. Cut the photocopied swatches apart, and arrange them in order from light to dark. Now the values will be very easy to see. If two of your swatches look like they have the same color value, then make your decision about which fabric is lighter and which is darker by looking at the colors. You will use the numbers on the forms to identify the fabric order. Place your sorted swatches in a plastic organizer box.

### Method 2

For this method of finding the values of your fabrics, you will use the "Quilted Photo Xpress 1.0" software that you get by free download from my website. Just as in Method 1, you will cut a small piece of the fabrics you will be using to make your photo quilt. Use the form at the end of chapter 9, then tape one fabric piece in each of the boxes. Next you will scan the forms and open the file in the Quilted Photo Xpress 1.0 software and print your pattern. Your fabrics will be numbered and you will know if you are missing any values. Go to page 12 for a screen shot of how the sorted fabrics will look. The forms and details for using Quilted Photo Xpress 1.0 for this amazing method are all in chapter 9.

The method for using the free software, Quilted Photo Xpress 1.0 to determine the value of your fabrics is a little tricky, but I have developed another software called "Valuations" that simplifies the value sorting process even more. It sorts the fabrics instantly! See page 69 for information.

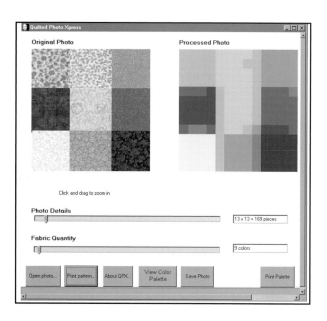

Balanced Photograph

Light Photograph

Dark Photograph

## Value Is The Key!

Once you have your fabrics in order by color value, your success is guaranteed! Not only is color value very important, it is even more important than the colors you choose! If you follow the instructions on page 56 to sort your fabrics, you will effortlessly create highlights, shadows, and depth in your quilted photograph.

## How To Choose A Great Photograph

The first rule that must be considered while choosing a photo is the light balance. It is ideal to have a balanced photograph that is not to light, or to dark. If the light areas of the image are really light, or if the dark areas are excessively dark, you will not be able to see the details of the image. If the image has a minor imbalance, it can be adjusted, but if the image is far out of balance, your quilt will not have clear details.

reading this section, you will be able to spot a good photo or a bad photo for Quilted Photography.

A great photo to use for Quilted Photography of a person or any other object has one light source. The light should come from one side, not from a flash on the top of the camera. A flash on the camera will shine a strong light on the front of the face of a person, washing away all of the shadows, details, and contours.

## How To Take Better Photographs

Although I am not a photography expert, I do know what kind of photographs work best for Quilted Photography.

Digital cameras are so simple to use, and the processing time is cut down to almost zero. It is possible to take better photos for quilting, as long as you have the right instruction. After

A better way to create the right kind of light is to sit by a window. The light will shine in from one direction and you can see the results before you even take the photo. If the shadow is not dark enough, get a dark cardboard or piece of fabric and hold it on the side of the subject that the shadow should be. The darkness of the cardboard will absorb the extra light.

Another way to get great light is to go out side and use the early morning or the late afternoon sun. A good rule to follow is take your photos before 10am or after 2pm. The mid-day sun will wash away all of the shadows, details, and contours.

For each of these lighting tips, pay attention to how the light is shining on your subject, and move around until you like how the light is shining on your subject.

Remember that shadows and light are equally important. When you include both shadow and light in your photos the quilts will be well balanced and pleasing.

The photograph below is a good example of the light source coming from one side and it has interesting shadows.

# Chapter 2

## Photocopy/Color Value Swatch Form

IMPORTANT NOTES: Copy must be grayscale so that you can see the values in varying shades of gray. First photocopy these forms, then attach your fabric swatches to the squares with tape or glue. Cut out the photocopied swatches. Arrange them in order by color value.

Cut Out Photocopies On Dotted Line

Attach Fabric Swatch Here
1

Attach Fabric Swatch Here
5

Attach Fabric Swatch Here
9

Attach Fabric Swatch Here
2

Attach Fabric Swatch Here
6

Attach Fabric Swatch Here
10

Attach Fabric Swatch Here
3

Attach Fabric Swatch Here
7

Attach Fabric Swatch Here
11

Attach Fabric Swatch Here
4

Attach Fabric Swatch Here
8

Attach Fabric Swatch Here
12

# Preparing The Fabrics And Patterns

## In this chapter

- Rules for choosing fabrics to create texture
- About the fabrics
- How to prepare and organize fabrics
- Fabric Cutting Tips
- Size and scale
- How to read the patterns
- Grid Guides and how to use them
- About the stabilizers

This is by far the most important chapter of this book. You must understand this chapter to understand the technique chapters that will follow.

## Rules For Choosing Fabrics To Create Texture

While choosing the fabrics for the textured techniques, you have to consider the backside of the fabrics. You must consider the backside because it will show. Each technique involves cutting through layers of fabric and making the cut edges curl away from the surface. With the edges of the fabrics moving away from the surface, you'll see the front of the fabric and also the back. The most important thing to remember while choosing your fabrics is that the backs and the fronts of the fabrics will both be visible.

## About The Fabrics

<u>Hand dyed and batik fabrics</u> - I used hand dyed fabrics in the book "More Amazing Quilted Photography" and I am using them again in this book because they are beautiful and the backsides of the fabrics are as beautiful as the fronts. This fabric is very flat and is not textural at all. You will create the texture with the techniques in the next 4 chapters. Here are three rules you must observe while choosing Batik and hand dyed fabrics for quilted photography.

Rule #1
Only use fabrics that have a consistent color value. If the hand dyed fabrics have more than one color, they must be in the same value family. For example if the fabric has light colors, all of the colors in the fabric must be in the light range of color.

Rule #2
Avoid tie dyed fabrics. They usually have big splotches of highly contrasting colors. Tie-dyes are usually not suitable because the color value can change drastically from one area of the yardage to another.

Rule #3
Try to choose batiks that have a small pattern and that read as solids as much as possible.

<u>Homespun fabrics</u> - Do you know what homespun fabrics are? I am using this term to refer to fabrics that are woven with yarns of different color to create a pattern. Since the colored yarns are what create the stripes or plaids, the pattern is exactly the same on the front and the back of the fabric. Another great thing about the homespun fabrics is they are loosely woven, and easily fluff to create texture.

<u>Flannel</u> - I have just begun to consider using flannel. I attend many quilt shows a year and I have seen many flannel quilts over the last few years. I never thought it was useful for Quilted Photography, but as I started researching fabrics for this book, this fabric choice became obvious. It is the same on both sides and it highly textured all by its self!

## How To Prepare And Organize Fabrics

If I am making a quilt for a bed, I always wash the fabrics before beginning. I do this because the quilt will be used, soiled and washed often

For quilted photography, most of the time, I do not wash the fabrics because the quilt will never be washed. But, because you will be wetting the fabrics to make the textures emerge, you should wash your fabrics before you begin. Washing will remove any excess dye for hand dyed fabrics and any remaining shrinkage for other fabrics.

After washing and ironing your fabrics, you will cut and prepare the fabric according to the technique instructions. Please pay careful attention to the preparation instructions because each technique is totally different from all of the rest.

After you have cut all your fabrics, make sure to place them in order from light to dark in your fabric organizer. Then number them with #1 being the lightest color. This organizer box will prevent you from losing any swatches, and it will also keep the fabrics labeled. To label the compartments, just use a permanent marker to write the number directly in each of the spaces or little labels work well too.

What if I run out of one of my fabrics?
If you miscalculate your yardage needs and run out of a fabric you can substitute with another fabric. Since the quilt has so many fabrics no one will ever notice the substitution. The rule for substituting fabrics is it has to have a color value that is darker than the fabric before it and lighter in value than the fabric after it.

## Size And Scale

Now you must cut your fabric. The techniques described in this book will use strips and squares. Refer to the preparation instruction in chapters to get the correct size and scale of the fabrics. The size of the fabric pieces has been tested and formulated to make the textures. Do not alter the sizes because the technique may not work properly.

while choosing the size of your finished quilt, you must consider where the quilt will be displayed when it is finished. The number of fabric pieces will determine the distance that will be required to see the photo image. The fewer pieces your quilt has, the more distance will be required to see the image clearly. The more pieces you quilt has, less distance will be required to see the image. You have complete control of the amount of fabric pieces when you use the free software, Quilted Photo Xpress 1.0 (go to www.QuiltedPhoto.com to get your free software).

To cut the squares and strips, I recommend that you use a rotary cutter, ruler and mat. When you cut your fabric please use all the safety precautions and methods described by the manufacturers of the equipment.

I use a special ruler with a lip on the edge that makes cutting accurate shapes very easy. The lip guide keeps the ruler perfectly straight while cutting. I also use a handle on my ruler. The handle allows me to apply pressure to the layers of fabric. The applied pressure keeps the fabrics from moving while cutting.

To learn about this special ruler and accessories, please go to page 77 to learn how you can get them. note: I usually cut 1/8th of a yard of each fabric in my palette to begin with. If you start with more then that, you may have a lot of wasted fabric.

## Fabric Cutting Tips

1. First fold your fabric in half with the salvage edges of the fabric together as shown.

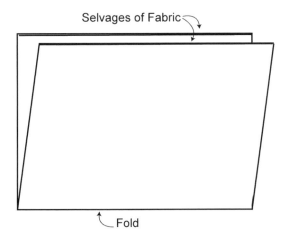

Selvages of Fabric

Fold

2. Now fold the fabric in half again matching the salvage edges to the folded edge.

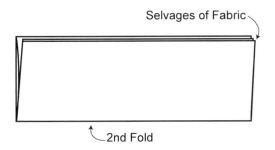

Selvages of Fabric

2nd Fold

3. Using your rotary cutter and mat, cut strips the desired width. To make accurate strips, I use the guidelines on the cutting mat as well as the lines on the ruler.

Use a rotary cutter and mat to cut strips the width of your squares

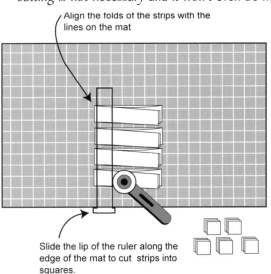

Slide the lip of the ruler along the edge of the mat to cut stright lines.

Align the fold of the fabric with the lines on the mat

4. Place the folded edge of the fabric on a guideline on the cutting mat as shown. Now if your ruler has a lip on the bottom, you will be able to slide it along the straight edge of the cutting mat to help you cut with accuracy. This process will go quickly once you get the hang of it.

5. To cut squares, place the strips horizontally on the cutting mat, following the lines of the cutting mat. Now slide the ruler along the bottom edge of the mat to cut your strips into squares. Cutting rectangles is almost the same as cutting squares. Just cut the pieces with one side longer than the width of the strip. Don't worry about making perfect your pieces ecaxtly perfect, just do the best you can and you will make a fantastic quilt. Perfection in your cutting is not necessary and it won't even be noticed!

Align the folds of the strips with the lines on the mat

Slide the lip of the ruler along the edge of the mat to cut strips into squares.

# Chapter 3

## How To Read The Patterns

The photo pattern includes your photo, the file name, number of squares in your pattern, the number of fabrics you have chosen and the finished quilt size. The pattern also includes the number of fabric pieces needed for each fabric you choose. (the patterns can be made with the free software Quilted Photo Xpress 1.0, go to www.QuiltedPhoto.com to get your free copy)

Note: the fabric choices are organized from light to dark with #1 being the lightest and the highest number being the darkest. The last and most important part of the pattern is the pattern grid. It contains all of the numbered boxes that will create your photographic quilt. On each page you will find row and column information so that you can tape the complete pattern together as shown in this diagram.

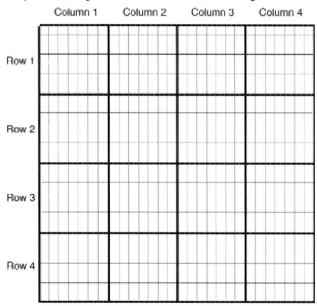

Fabric Requirement Chart
This chart will help you approximate the amount of fabric you will need. It tells the amount of squares you can cut out of 1/16th, 1/8th, 1/4 and 1/2 yard. These estimates are only for squares, but you will be able to get an idea of what you will need for strips as well.

### The Color Palette
You will notice that the Color Palette is always arranged in order, with #1 being the lightest color and the highest number being the darkest.

### The Pattern Grid
The last and most important part of the pattern is the Pattern Grid. Each Pattern Grid contains numbered squares that correspond with your sorted and numbered fabrics. If you are using the free software to create your pattern, you will also need grid guides to use the pattern. Read the next section to learn what a grid guide is and how to use it. If you have any of the other versions of Quilted Photo software you can skip over the next section, grid guides are not needed because the grids and numbers are printed in full size from your printer.

## Grid Guides And How To Use Them

The grid guide is a printed grid. The grids are the correct sizes needed to make the quilts described in the "Quilted Photography" books. Transfer the numbers from the Pattern Grid to the Grid Guide. Use a soft pencil to write the numbers into the grid (3B soft pencil). The soft lead is dark enough to see through the interfacing and it is easy to erase. I also recommend taping several grid guides together to make the correct size you will need for your project without erasing numbers.

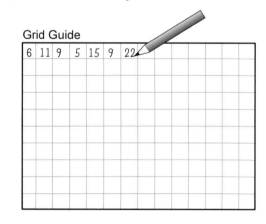

Grid Guide

|  | 1/16th yard | 1/8th yard | ¼ yard | ½ yard |
|---|---|---|---|---|
| 1" squares | 94 | 188 | 376 | 752 |
| 1 ¼" squares | 55 | 110 | 220 | 440 |
| 1 ½" squares | 46 | 92 | 184 | 368 |
| 2" squares | 23 | 46 | 92 | 184 |

To use the grid guide, place it under the appropriate stabilizer (adhesive side facing up) for the technique you are using. The stabilizer will hold all of the fabrics together so that you can stitch them according to the instructions for the technique you have chosen.

Place grid guide on the table

| 8 | 4 | 2 | 4 | 9 | 5 | 3 | 9 | 3 | 2 | 11 | 4 | 3 | 4 |
|---|---|---|---|---|---|---|---|---|---|----|---|---|---|
| 5 | 8 | 4 | 2 | 4 | 9 | 5 | 3 | 9 | 3 | 2 | 11 | 4 | 3 |
| 4 | 2 | 4 | 9 | 5 | 3 | 9 | 3 | 2 | 11 | 4 | 3 | 1 | 1 |
| 8 | 4 | 2 | 4 | 9 | 5 | 3 | 9 | 3 | 2 | 11 | 4 | 3 | 4 |
| 5 | 8 | 4 | 2 | 4 | 9 | 5 | 3 | 9 | 3 | 2 | 11 | 4 | 3 |
| 4 | 2 | 4 | 9 | 5 | 3 | 9 | 3 | 2 | 11 | 4 | 3 | 1 | 1 |
| 8 | 4 | 2 | 4 | 9 | 5 | 3 | 9 | 3 | 2 | 11 | 4 | 3 | 4 |
| 5 | 8 | 4 | 2 | 4 | 9 | 5 | 3 | 9 | 3 | 2 | 11 | 4 | 3 |
| 4 | 2 | 4 | 9 | 5 | 3 | 9 | 3 | 2 | 11 | 4 | 3 | 1 | 1 |
| 8 | 4 | 2 | 4 | 9 | 5 | 3 | 9 | 3 | 2 | 11 | 4 | 3 | 4 |

Place fusible interfacing on top of the grid guide

If the pattern has a straight grid then put the guide under the interfacing the same way it appears. If you made your pattern on an angle then use the following instructions for positioning the grid guide.

Use 30 or 60 degree lines on you ruler to mark fusible interfacing. This line is a guid' for your grid guide if your pattern is on an angle.

Interfacing

You will need a quilting ruler that has 30 degree or 60 degree markings on it. Line up the 30 or 60 degree angle with the straight edge of the interfacing as shown in the diagram A.

Mark a 30 degree line as shown in the diagram. Next you will line up the edge of the grid with the angled line you have drawn (diagram B).

If you made your pattern on an angle other than 30 or 60 degree, then match the angle of your pattern for this step.

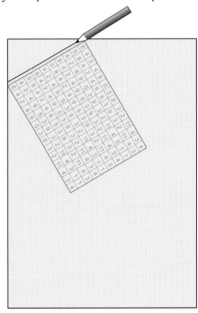

## About The Stabilizers

All of the "Quilted Photo" techniques us some sort of stabilizer or interfacing to hold all of the fabric pieces together. The stabilizers must be thin enough to see through (to read the numbers on the patterns) and must have an adhesive to stick the fabrics to it. To make the textured techniques in this book, the stabilizer must also have another important characteristic. The stabilizer needs to somehow, be removed after the fabrics are stitched in place. If not removed it will be visible, just as the backsides of the fabrics will be visible. The following stabilizer options have all the characteristics required for the textured techniques in this book.

# Chapter 3

1.      The first option is to use a clear water-soluble stabilizer with water-soluble sticky tape. This is the most budget conscious option and it is the option I will describe in the technique instructions.

2.      The second option is to use a product called "Free-Lace". This product is easy to use, but costs a lot more and is much harder to find then the above options. It is water-soluble and it is sticky on one side without using tape.

# Faux Chenille Technique

## In this chapter

◆ What is this technique?
◆ Fabrics suitable for technique
◆ Preparation Instructions
◆ Putting it together
◆ Stencils
◆ Possible Variations
◆ Examples

## What Is This Technique?

This technique is created with squares of fabric. The fabrics are assembled according to a quilted photo pattern to create a photo image. The assembled squares are cut to create the texture. After the fabrics are cut, the photo image is visible, but the squares seem to disappear!

## Fabrics Suitable For Technique

Hand dyed, batik and homespun fabrics all work well for the faux chenille techniques in this chapter.

## Preparation Instructions

For this technique, I had to consider size and scale. The size of the fabric pieces, the stitching being used and the scale of the pattern all had to be considered. follow the instructions closely.

When you prepare your pattern for this technique, use a pattern with 1¼" squares. Please make your pattern with 8 to 12 fabrics, this will make the number of fabrics you have to find easily manageable. You can use more fabrics if you like, but it is not necessary. The pattern will be either made with 'Quilted Photo Xpress 1.0' and grid guides or you can print your pattern with an upgraded version of 'Quilted Photo' software.

Cut your fabrics into 1¼" squares. Instructions for cutting and organizing the fabrics were explained in chapter 3. Please refer to chapter 3 for those details.

## Putting It Together

For the chenille technique, first you will assemble 1¼" squares of fabrics according to the "Quilted Photo" pattern of your choice. Lay the pattern on the table first then the water-soluble stabilizer on top of it. The squares of fabric will be adhered to water-soluble stabilizer with water-soluble tape as shown below.

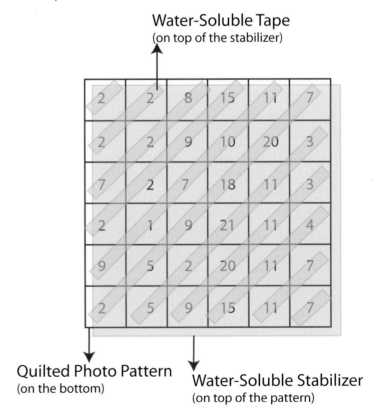

**Water-Soluble Tape**
(on top of the stabilizer)

**Quilted Photo Pattern**
(on the bottom)

**Water-Soluble Stabilizer**
(on top of the pattern)

Make sure your pattern is secure on the table you are working on. A little scotch tape on each corner will keep the pattern from moving. Peel the paper off of the water-soluble tape and place the squares of fabric according to the numbers. You will notice that the fabric squares are bigger than the squares of the

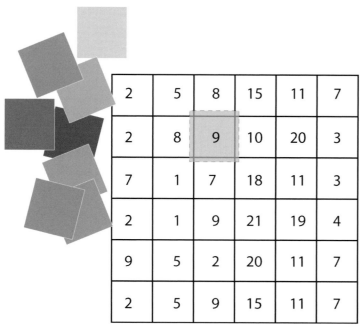

| 2 | 5 | 8 | 15 | 11 | 7 |
|---|---|---|----|----|---|
| 2 | 8 | 9 | 10 | 20 | 3 |
| 7 | 1 | 7 | 18 | 11 | 3 |
| 2 | 1 | 9 | 21 | 19 | 4 |
| 9 | 5 | 2 | 20 | 11 | 7 |
| 2 | 5 | 9 | 15 | 11 | 7 |

will show through where the fabrics are slashed. Note: you can also add a batting and another backing after the four fabric layers to add stability. It is optional so I have not shown it in the diagram.

Third, you will stitch rows of straight stitching, through all of the layers, on the bias, ½' or 5/8" apart. I use a thread that is the same color as most of the squares but the thread will not show much in the end.

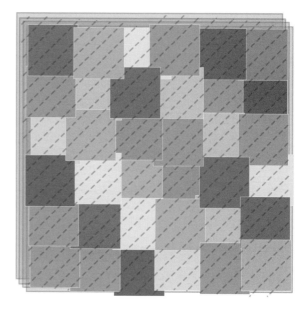

pattern. This is good, they will overlap a little as you can see in the above diagram.
Continue placing the fabric squares until the whole patern is finished.

Next, you will layer 4 whole fabric pieces of fabric under the quilt top. The fabric layers don't have to be in any particular order, just keep in mind, the last layer (the backing layer)

## Four Whole Pieces Of Fabric

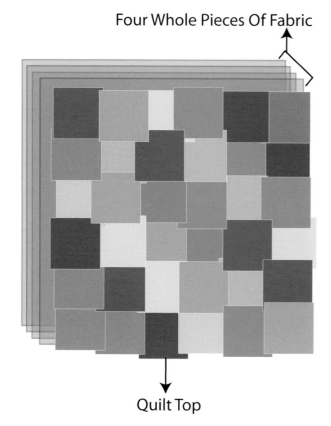

Quilt Top

Fourth, you will use scissors or a special chenille cutter to slash through the top 4 layers of fabric, preserving the bottom layer. You **must not cut through the back layer**. You will slash between each row of stitching.

After cutting the layers, brush the exposed layers of fabric with a chenille brush. Wash the quilt in the washing machine. It is a good idea to place the quilt inside an old pillowcase while washing. This will contain all of the lint/threads and keep them from clogging your plumbing. You will notice that the water-soluble stabilizer has totally disappeared!

While the quilt is still wet, brush the exposed edges again to fluff them even more. Lastly, place the quilt in the dryer. Dry the quilt in the dryer until it is most of the way dry, allow it to finish by lying flat on a table and air drying.

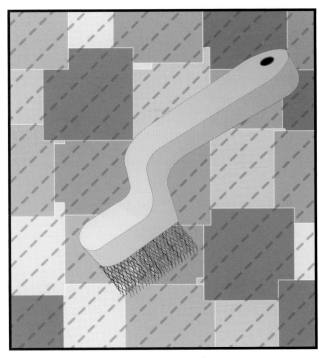

## Stencils

An awesome way to make your quilt more beautiful is to use stencils for the stitching pattern! I had never used a stencil before but it hit me like a ton of bricks that I could just trace a beautiful pattern on my chenille quilts and follow the lines with my sewing machine! I really love this idea.

To choose a stencil, you need to make sure it has rows of stitching and that it has a pattern that is primarily set on the bias. The rows also have to be ½' to 5/8" apart. This option will give you wonderful new possibilities for your chenille design! Here are some of the easy stencil designs I have used.

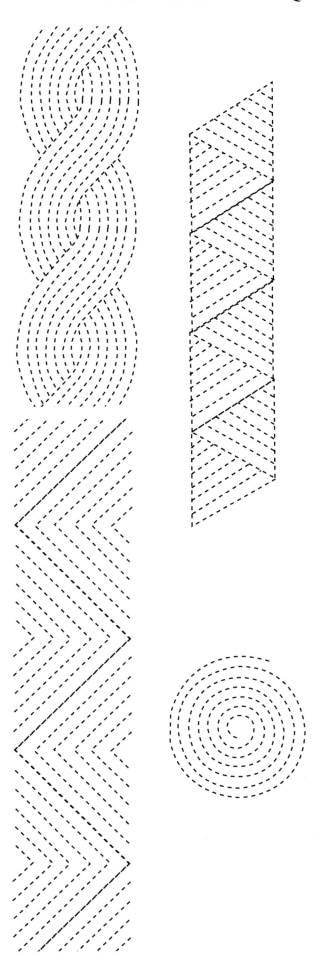

These stencils are all traditional stencils, inexpensive and are easy to find. I like using the border patterns. They may not look inspiring alone but when you put them together for chenille this is what you get!

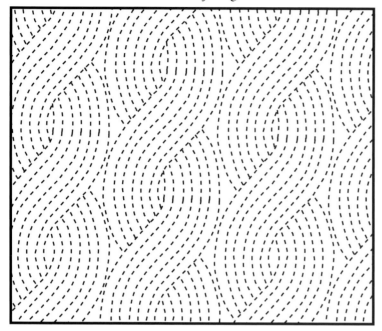

This cable pattern is what I used for the waterfall quilt you will see later in this chapter.

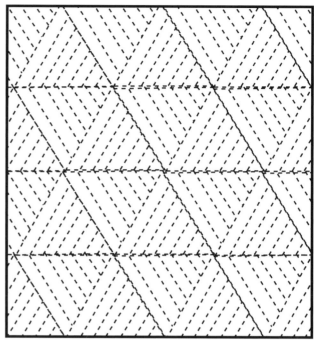

The triangles above and the spirals below are also lovely and interesting options for chenille patterns to apply to your quilt top.

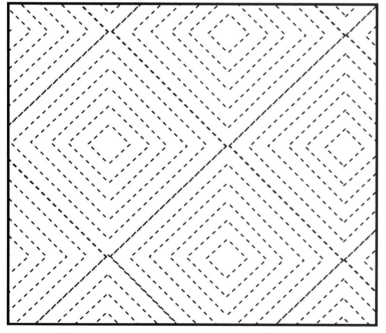

This pattern was made with the stencil in the lower center of the previous page. It is versital and can make other formations by how you line up the design.

To use stencils you will need to add an additional layer of water-soluble stabilizer to the top of the quilt before stitching. This top layer will hold all of the squares down tight and secure. and it will give you a place to draw the stencil pattern! This extra layer will make stitching the rows easier because the fabric squares will not move around. The water-soluble stabilizer is applied with quilt basting spray.

The stencil pattern is then drawn on the stabilizer with a marker. I use a normal black sharpie to mark the pattern onto the top layer of water-soluble stabilizer. The kind of marker you use will depend on the stabilizer you use

on the top. Test the marker and stabilizer together to make sure the ink does not bleed through the stabilizer and stain you quilt. Remember the stabilizer and the ink will wash away when the quilt is wet.

Note: When you use stencils, the ends of the rows don't always come to the edge of the quilt, you have to work a little harder to cut the layers and preserve the back layer, but the results are really worth it! I use small sharp scissors to cut the layers when I use stencils.

After cutting the layers, brush the exposed layers of fabric with a chenille brush. Wash the quilt in the washing machine. It is a good idea

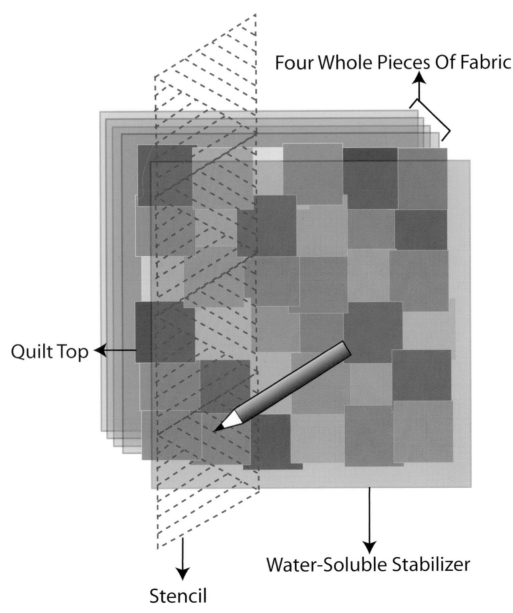

Four Whole Pieces Of Fabric

Quilt Top

Water-Soluble Stabilizer

Stencil

to place the quilt inside an old pillowcase while washing. This will contain all of the lint/threads and keep them from clogging your plumbing. You will notice that the water-soluble stabilizer has totally disappeared! While the quilt is still wet, brush the exposed edges again to fluff them even more. Lastly, place the quilt in the dryer. Dry the quilt in the dryer until it is most of the way dry, allow it to finish by lying flat on a table and air drying.

Here is a great source for the stencils described in this chapter.

**JD Stencils**
PO Box 758
Cadiz KY 42211
270-924-3434
http://www.jdstencils.com

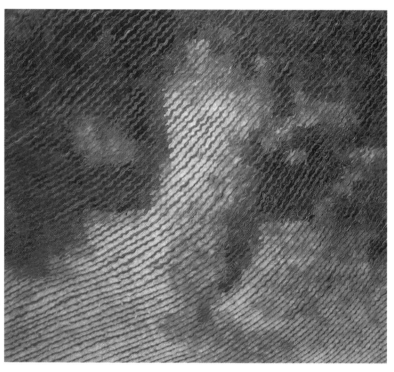

## Possible Variation

Another simple variation is to change the angle of the pattern. It is a simple change that will have big impact. Changing the angle of the pattern will change the direction of the chenille rows. Liz Joe changed the direction of the pattern to a 45 degree angle and her chenille rows are straight up and down. You can see her quilt on the next page. Remember, the stitched rows always have to be on the bias grain of the fabrics to fluff up and make chenille texture.

### Fancy Kitty

This quilt was the first chenille quilt I made. It is made using the most basic faux chenille technique. I have included a photograph of the quilt before it was slashed and the photo above is after it is finished. My friend Jan Emmanuel helped me make it.

### Remembering Royse at 3

This quilt was made by Liz joe   38 1/4" x 45 1/2"
Liz made this wonderful quilt  (her grandson Royse) in the basic faux chenille technique but she turned the pattern on point so that the chenille rows would be straight up and down.  Liz also accidently poked holes through the back layer of fabric.....so she printed fabric photos and covered all the holes! She is my kind of girl! Thanks Liz


Hi Tammie,
Thank you so much for letting me a part of this book.  My friends think I need to have a book signing party when it comes out. (for one page) That shows you how undistinguished our careers have been!  Oh well, we've had a lot of fun even if this is the closest any of us have ever gotten to being published and famous!
Liz

## Duncan

This quilt was made for Quilter's News Network (see page 60). This was also the first time I tried using the homespun fabrics to make a chenille photo quilt. If you look closely, you'll see the checkerboard chenille pattern.... stencils are really cool and I hope you try using them!

## Cabled Gradation

Do you want to make a quilt that is a little more abstract? Well this is a gradation from light to dark that is made more interesting with a stencil pattern for the chenille. If you want the gradation image below or one of the others I have prepared for you, download it at:
www.QuiltedPhoto.com/indexfree.html
Enter password: 96985314

# Customer Photos

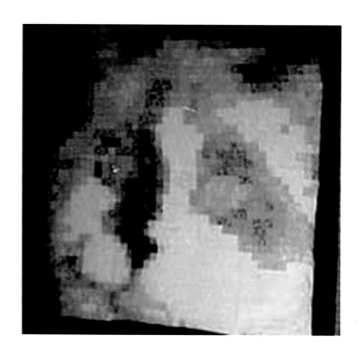

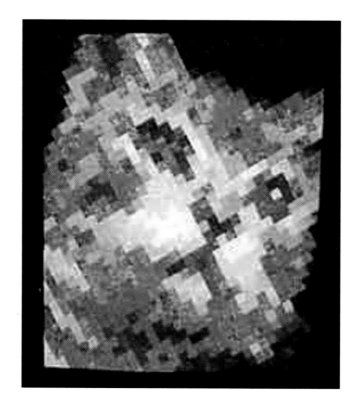

# Layered Chenille Technique

### In this chapter

- ◆ What is this technique?
- ◆ Fabrics suitable for technique
- ◆ Preparation Instructions
- ◆ Putting it together
- ◆ Possible Variations
- ◆ Examples
- ◆ Sample Pattern

## What Is This Technique?

This technique is created with squares of fabric. One layer of large squares with another layer of smaller squares on top of it.The fabrics are assembled to create a photo image then stitched through the centers of each square horizontally and vertically. The center stitching holds the centers of the squares down but leaves the corners free. Brush the corners with the chenille brush to create texture and reveal some of the under layer of fabrics You don't see the whole bottom layer, it just peeks through at the corners to let you see a a bit of the bottom image.

## Fabrics Suitable For Technique

Hand dyed, batik and homespun fabrics all work well for the Layered Chenille technique in this chapter.

## Preparation Instructions

For this technique, I had to consider size and scale. The size of the fabric pieces, the stitching being used and the scale of the pattern all had to be considered to make it work.

You will prepare two patterns for this technique. The patterns will have different square sizes but the finished size of each layer will be the same. To do this you will have to do a little math. Example: if you make the first pattern with I" squares, you can make the

second pattern with 4" squares or even 3" squares. You will have to do a little math to determine the amount of photo detail needed to make both patterns have the same finished size.

I would use the pattern above for the first layer. It has a lot of detail at 40 x 40 squares. The total amount of squares is 1600 and I" squares would be perfect.

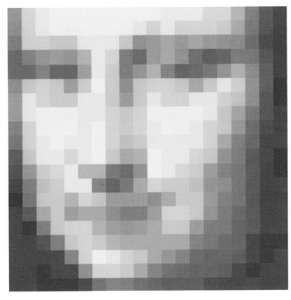

For the second layer, I would use 2" squares and to make the the second layer match the first layer in finished size I divided the amount of squares by 2 to get a pattern that is

20 x 20 squares. The pattern is easy to make with any 'Quilted Photo' software.

Here are my suggestions:
If you will be using Quilted Photo Xpress 1.0 (free software) you will also need to use grid guides. Refer to page 18 for instruction on how to use grid guides. Look pn page 75 for coupons to get free grid guides.

If you are using an upgraded version of 'Quilted Photo' software, you will not need grid guides, you can print the patterns directly from your computer and printer.

Please make your pattern with 8 to 12 fabrics, this will make the amount of fabrics managable. You can use more fabrics if you like, but it is not necessary.

The squares for the top layer need to be exactly the same size as printed pattern. The squares should not overlap at all. The bigger squares for the second layer need to be a little bigger than the pattern. The squares need to overlap so the whole background is covered.

Cut your fabrics according to the Instructions explained in chapter 3.

## Putting It Together

For the layered chenille technique, you will assemble the two layers seperatly. Place the squares of fabric according to the "Quilted Photo" patterns.

For the top layer, the squares of fabric will be adhered to water-soluble stabilizer with water-soluble tape as seen in the previous column.

For the second layer, use a regular stabilizer like Fusible Tricot or lightweight fusible Interfacing. Place the fabric squares according to the pattern then iron them to fuse them to the fusible stabilizer. I also like Steam-A-Seam2 as the stabilizer for the bottom layer. If you use Steam-A-Seam2, you will not need to use the iron to adhear the squares to the stabilizer because it is sticky all by itself. note with Steam-A-Seam2 you must not iron the squares until the the batting is under it.

Fabrics for bottom layer are placed with a 1/4" overlap

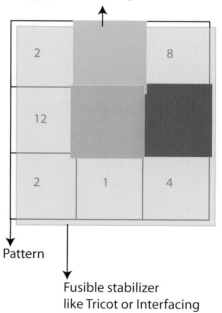

Pattern

Fusible stabilizer
like Tricot or Interfacing

Fabrics for top layer are placed side by side with no overlap

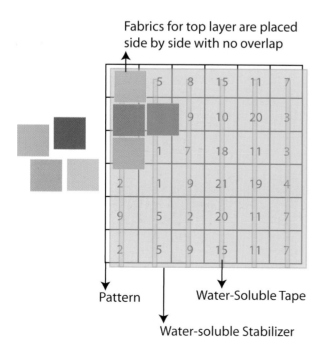

Pattern

Water-Soluble Tape

Water-soluble Stabilizer

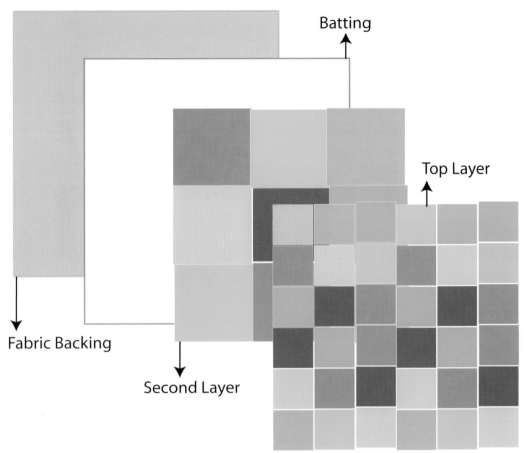

Batting

Top Layer

Fabric Backing

Second Layer

After completing both of the photo layers, you will place your backing first, batting second, the layer with the bigger squares then add the layer with the smaller squares on the top.

Third, you will stitch rows of straight stitching, through all of the layers. Stitch through the center of each square vertically and horizontally. The center stitching holds the centers of the squares down but leaves the corners free.

After sewing all of the rows in both directions, put the whole quilt into the washing machine. It is a good idea to place the quilt inside an old pillowcase while washing. This will contain all of the lint/threads and keep them from clogging your plumbing. You will notice that the water-soluble stabilizer has totally disappeared! While the quilt is still wet, brush the exposed edges to fluff them and create the texture. Lastly, place the quilt in the dryer. Dry the quilt in the dryer until it is most of the way dry, allow it to finish by lying flat on a table and air drying.

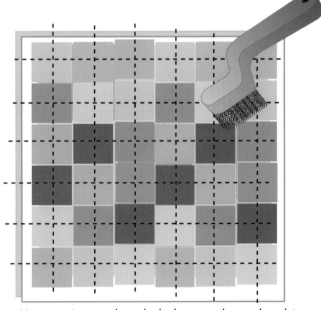

You won't see the whole bottom layer, but bits of it peek through where the corners are raised up. You will have two virsion of the same photograph on two layers showing at once. I have only done this technique with one photo, but it may also work using two different photos for the layers. I will be testing this and putting the results in my newsletter.

## Possible Variations

An interesting variation for this technique is to cut the top squares on the bias. The bias edges of the exposed corners will make a different texture than the straight cut squares. This is a subtle change but I like it a lot.

I really like this type of quilt with a border. A border makes the quilt have a polished finish.

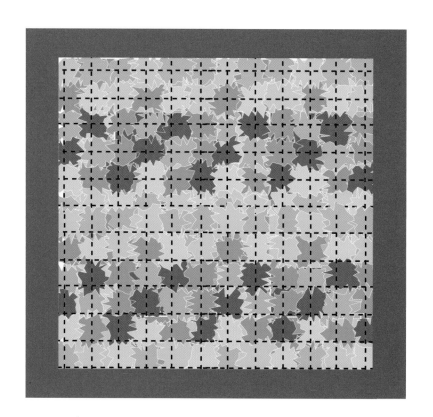

Photograph by Zoza & Fabric by Starr Fabrics

## Abstract Tulips

For this example I have decided to make an image that is kind of abstract. I have chosen a close-up view of a flower because I wanted to capture the graceful movement of the petals and the subtle changes in color that only nature can create. I used the leftover squares from the second layer to make a border that go from light to dark.

## Sample pattern

Pattern for top layer

```
22 22 22 22 22 22 22 20 20 20 20 20 20 18 18  8  6  6 15 15  6  6  8  7 10 10 10 10 10 10 11
22 22 22 22 22 22 22 20 20 20 20 20 20 18 16 15 15 13 15 15  6  8  8 10 10 10 10 10 11 11
22 22 22 22 22 23 22 22 20 20 20 20 18 18 15 15 15 15 15 15  6  8 12 10 10 10 11 10 11 11
22 22 23 23 23 23 23 23 20 18 18 18 16 16 15 15 15 15 15 15  8 12 12 10 10 10 10 11 10 10
22 23 23 23 23 23 23 23 20 18 12 12 16 15 15 15 15 15 15 15 15 12 12 10 10 10 11 10 10
22 23 23 23 23 23 22 23 18 12 12 12  8 15 15 15 15 15 15 15 16 12 12 10 10 10 11 11 11 10
20 23 23 23 21 22 22 23 18 12 10  7  8  8  8 16 16 15 15 16 16 12 12 10 10 10 11 11 11  7
19 21 23 23 21 22 22 21 18 10  7  7  7  7 12 12 12 15 16 16 16 12 12 10 10 11 11 11 11  3
19 19 21 21 21 22 22 21 18  7  7 12 12 12 12 12 12 16 16 16 16 12 12 10 11 11 11 11  2
17 19 21 21 21 23 19 12  7 12 22 17 11 14 12 12 12 12 12 12 12 12 12 11 11 11 10  2
17 17 19 21 21 19 23 21 12 10 17 22 20 14 14 12 12 12  7  7 12 12 12 12 12 11 11 10  3  2
19 19 21 21 21 19 19 21 19 17 19 22 17 14 14 14 12 10  7  7  8 12 18 18 12 12 10  3  2  3
19 20 22 22 23 19 19 19 19 19 17 17 14 14 14 14 10 10  7  7 12 12 16 12 12 12  6  2  2  3
19 19 19 22 23 21 19 17 19 21 19 17 17 14 14 11 10 10 10 12 12 16 16 16  6  6  5  5  5  5
19 19 19 21 22 21 17 19 21 21 17 17 17 14 14 17 14 12 12 12 16 15 13  9  9  9  5  5  5  5
19 19 19 19 21 21 23 21 21 19 17 14 19 22 22 20 12 12 15 15 13 13 13  9  9  9  5  5  5  5
19 19 19 19 21 21 24 21 21 21 19 17 17 20 18 18 16 16 15 15 13 13 13  9  9  5  5  5  5  5
19 19 21 21 23 24 21 20 22 21 17 12 12 12 18 18 16 16 15 15 13 13 13  9  9  5  5  5  5  5
17 17 19 22 22 19 23 24 20 20 17 12 12 12 12 12 12 16 15 15 13 13  9  9  5  5  5  5  6
17 19 22 21 21 19 17 17 14 17 14  7  7 12 12 12 12 12 15 15 13 13  9  5  5  5  5  6  6
21 21 21 19 19 19 17 14 14 14 14 14 10 12 12 12 16 15 15 13 13  9  5  5  5  5  6  8  8
19 19 19 19 19 17 10 11 11 14 14 14 14 12 12 16 15 15 13 13 13  9  9  9  6  8  8  4
19 19 19 19 17 12 10 11 11 11 14 14 14 11 11 12 15 15 15 15  8 12 12 10 10 10 10
19 19 19 19 17  7  7  7 11 11 14 14 14 11 10 10 12 12 16 16 16 16 12 12 10 10 10 10 10
19 19 19 19 17  4  7  7 10 11 11 11 14 12 12 12 12 16 18 18 18 12 12 12 10 10 10  7  7
21 21 19 17  8  4  7  7  7  7 11 11 12 18 18 18 16 18 18 18 12 12 12 10 10 10  7  7  7
23 23 21 12  3  4  4  4  4  7  7 10 16 16 16 16 18 16 12 12 12 10 10 10 10  7 10 10 10
23 23 18  8  4  4  4  4  3  6  8 15 15 16 16 16 16 12 12 12 10 10 10  7  7  7  7 10 10
22 22 18  8  8  4  3  6  6 13 13 15 15 15 15 15 12 12 10 10 10 10 10 10 10 10 10 10 10
22 20 18 12  8  8  8  8  6 13 13 13 15 15 15  6  8  8 12 10 10 10 10 10 10 10 10 10 10  7
```

Pattern for second layer

| 22 | 22 | 18 | 15 | 10 | 10 |
|----|----|----|----|----|----|
| 23 | 22 | 7  | 12 | 12 | 11 |
| 19 | 19 | 14 | 12 | 12 | 5  |
| 19 | 21 | 17 | 16 | 13 | 5  |
| 19 | 11 | 14 | 15 | 13 | 10 |
| 23 | 4  | 15 | 12 | 10 | 10 |

## Pattern Details

Finished Quilt Size = 27' x 27"
Materials Needed:
- 1/8 yd of 24 hand dyed fabrics with values from light to dark color value in warm colors.
- Cut 30% of each fabric into ¾" squares, cut 30% into 4" squares, cut the remaining 30% into 3" squares. Pre-wash your fabrics.

Also prepare: 4 - 3" x 28" strips Coordinating Backing Fabric
·        1 - 26" x 26" Coordinating Backing Fabric
·        4 - 2.5" x 28" strips Cotton Batting
·        1 - 26" x 26" Cotton Batting

Sample Single Color Palette  (see page 10)

| 1  | 2  | 3  | 4  | 5  | 6  | 7  | 8  |
|----|----|----|----|----|----|----|----|
| 9  | 10 | 11 | 12 | 13 | 14 | 15 | 16 |
| 17 | 18 | 19 | 20 | 21 | 22 | 23 | 24 |

# Rag Chenille Technique

## In this chapter

- ◆ What is this technique?
- ◆ Fabrics suitable for technique
- ◆ Preparation Instructions
- ◆ Putting it together
- ◆ Possible Variations
- ◆ Examples
- ◆ Sample Pattern

## What Is This Technique?

This technique is created with layers and strips of fabric. The strips are applied in a vertical pattern and then the strips are also stitched vertically with the seams exposed on the outside of the quilt. The patterns are made with of rectangular shape instead of squares. The shape is rectangular because seam allowances in needed on two sides and none is needed on the top and bottom. The seam allowances are clipped to create a fringe or rag effect.

## Fabrics Suitable For Technique

Hand dyed, batik, flannel and homespun fabrics all work well for the techniques in this chapter.

## Preparation Instructions

For the rag technique, you will need to make you pattern with a 1¼" or a 1½" by ½" rectangular pattern. The pattern can be made with the Rag Grid Guide (See the conclusion at the end of the book for instructions for getting grid guides for free! ) or printed, automatically with Quilted Photo Xpress 3.0 or higher.

To prepare the fabrics, look at your fabric usage chart to see how much of each fabric you will need, and double that amount. I suggest that you make your quilts with 8 to 12 fabrics. You can use more fabrics if you

like but it is not necessary. Make a double layer of each fabric by spraying the fabric with quilt basting spray and folding in half.

Next, cut the fabrics into 1¼" or 1½" strips, on the straight grain. The width of the fabric strips should match the pattern you created.

Instructions for cutting and organizing the fabrics were explained in chapter 3. Please refer to chapter 3 for these details.

## Putting It Together

For the rag technique, first place your pattern on a table. Second place the water-soluble stabilizer on top of the pattern, then place a row of water-soluble tape down the center of each vertical row.

The strips are applied in a vertical pattern, following the numbers to create the photo image. It is important to make the strips overlap vertically (at least 1/4") where the fabric changes. This is to make sure there are no holes in the quilt when you wash away the stabilizer.

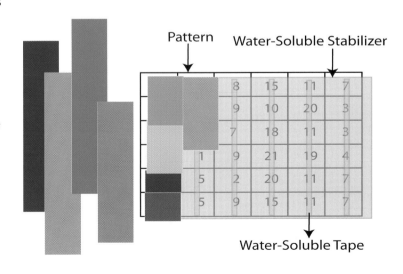

Pattern    Water-Soluble Stabilizer

Water-Soluble Tape

Stitch the vertical seams with 3/8th inch seam allowance if your strips are 1¼". Stitch the vertical seams with ½" seam allowance if your strips are 1½" wide. Stitch the seam allowance so that the seams are exposed on the right side of the quilt.

**Fold back each row with the seam on the outside and stitch vertically as shown**

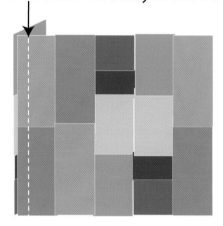

The next step is to clip all of the seam allowances every 1/4 inch. Clipping the seam allowances will create a fringe or rag effect. Avoid cutting the stitching.

If you want to put a backing and batting on this quilt, this is the time to do it. Iron the quilt top flat. Then layer the batting and backing fabric under the quilt top. Move the seam to the side and stitch through all of the layers following the stitching line. Stitch a vertical row of quilting about every 3 rows.

The last step for this technique is to wash the quilt in the washing machine. It is a good idea to place the quilt inside an old pillowcase while washing. This will contain all of the lint/threads and keep them from clogging your plumbing. You will notice that the water-soluble stabilizer has totally disappeared! While the quilt is still wet, brush the exposed edges with a chenille brush to fluff the frayed edges. Lastly, place the quilt in the dryer. Dry the quilt in the dryer until it is most of the way dry, allow it to finish by lying flat on a table and air drying.

## Possible Variations

### Variation 1
Prepare your fabrics with more than one fused layers of fabric. Use quilt basting spray to fuse the fabrics together before cutting your strips. Adding two or three layers will make the texture fluffier.

### Variation 2
Change the angle of the pattern. It is a simple change that will have a have big impact on the look of the finished quilt. Changing the angle of the pattern to 45 degrees will cause the direction of the rows to turn 45 degrees also.

### Variation 3
Cut your strips on the bias. This will make the texture really fluffy.

**Mona Again**

**Customer Photos**

# Stacked Strip Chenille Technique

## In this chapter

◆ What is this technique?
◆ Fabrics suitable for technique
◆ Preparation Instructions
◆ Putting it together
◆ Possible Variations
◆ Examples

## What Is This Technique

This technique is created with layers and strips of fabric. The strips are applied in vertical and horizontal directions. The strips are stitched down the center of each strip. After washing the quilt, the chenille texture is revealed.

## Fabrics Suitable For Technique

Hand dyed, batik and homespun fabrics all work well for the layered technique in this chapter.

## Preparation Instructions

For the stacked strip technique, I had to consider size and scale. The width of the fabric strip, stitching, how the fabric will behave and the scale of the pattern have all been considered. After conducting tests, I have determined the best pattern and fabric sizes to achieve the stacked strip technique.

When you prepare your pattern for this technique, use a pattern with ½" squares. Make your pattern with 8 to 12 fabrics, this will make the amount of fabrics you need to prepare managable. You can use more fabrics if you like, but it is not necessary. The pattern will be either printed from "Quilted Photo Xpress 3.0" or you can make your pattern with the free software (Quilted Photo Xpress 1.0) and Grid Guides.

To prepare the fabrics, look at your fabric usage chart to see how much of each fabric you will need, then double the amounts that are suggested. Use quilt basting spray to fuse two layers of each fabric together. First spray the fabric then fold it in half.

Next, cut the fabrics into ½" strips, on the bias.

Instructions for cutting and organizing the fabrics were explained in chapter 3. Please refer to chapter 3 for these details.

## Putting It Together

For the stacked strip technique, first place your pattern on a table. Second place the water-soluble stabilizer on top of the pattern, then place a row of water-soluble tape down the center of each row.

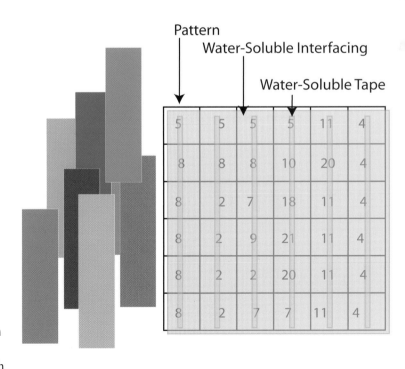

Pattern
Water-Soluble Interfacing
Water-Soluble Tape

| 5 | 5 | 5 | 5 | 11 | 4 |
| 8 | 8 | 8 | 10 | 20 | 4 |
| 8 | 2 | 7 | 18 | 11 | 4 |
| 8 | 2 | 9 | 21 | 11 | 4 |
| 8 | 2 | 2 | 20 | 11 | 4 |
| 8 | 2 | 7 | 7 | 11 | 4 |

Now, apply the strips of fabric according to the pattern, following the numbers to create the photo image. The strips of fabric will be adhered to water-soluble stabilizer, vertically, horizontally, or both. Apply the strips along a row if the numbers are matching. Continue until the whole quilt top is complete.

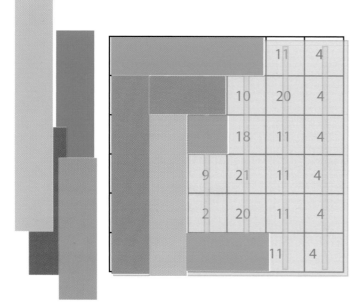

Next, layer the photo image, one layer of fabric, cotton batting and a backing.

Spray the top of the quilt with quilt basting spray and apply more water-soluble stabilizer on top. this layer will make stitching the strips much easier.

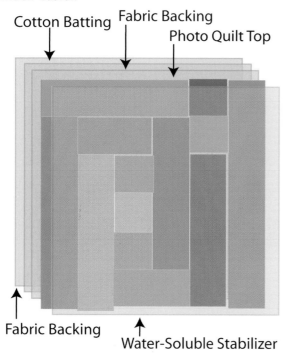

Cotton Batting    Fabric Backing
                  Photo Quilt Top

Fabric Backing    Water-Soluble Stabilizer

Now, stitch down the center of each fabric strip. Stitch all the way to the edges of the strips and back tack to secure it. Stitch through all of the layers. This stitching is easy if you have placed all of you fabrics vertically or horizontally. It will take a little more time if you have mixed directions, however it is worth the extra effort.

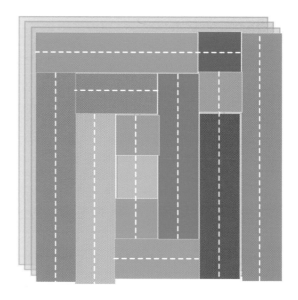

The last step for this technique is to wash the quilt in the washing machine. It is a good idea to place the quilt inside an old pillowcase while washing. This will contain all of the lint/threads and keep them from clogging your plumbing. You will notice that the water-soluble stabilizer has totally disappeared! While the quilt is still wet, brush the exposed edges again to fluff them even more.

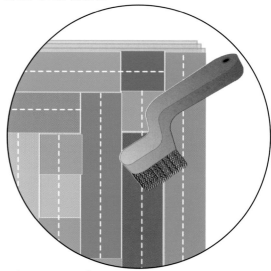

Lastly, place the quilt in the dryer. Dry the quilt in the dryer until it is most of the way dry, allow it to finish by lying flat on a table and air drying.

## Possible Variations

### Variation 1
Prepare your fabrics with four fused layers of fabric. using four layers will make the texture fluffier.

### Variation 2
Change the angle of the pattern. It is a simple change that will have a have big impact on the look of the finished quilt. Changing the angle of the pattern to 45 degrees will cause the direction of the stitching to turn 45 degrees also.

**Angie at 6**

In my first book I showed you quilts of my daughter Angela but that was 3 years ago! I thought it was time to make another quilt so you can see her now! This is made with the stacked strip method and it is not yet stitched and fluffed but you can see it on my website at www.QuiltedPhoto.com/indexfree.html Use password: 96985314

# Finishing Your Textured Quilt

## In this chapter

- Completing the project
- Trimming the quilt
- Adding borders
- Batting and backing
- Bindings
- How to display a quilted photo

## Completing the project

Even though you have made your amazing photographic quilt top, the project is not complete until you have made it suitable for display. There are many ways you can finish your quilt top. I will discuss each of the available options in this chapter. The options range from borders, to bindings, to stretching your quilt top like a canvas.

## Trimming the quilt

If you have placed all of your fabric pieces perfectly inside the lines, your quilt will finish with perfectly straight edges and squared corners. However this never happens and it is o.k. if your quilt is not perfect, you can trim the edges.

If you want to add a border to frame your quilt, trim the edges with your rotary cutter first. If you are just adding a binding to finish your quilt, then wait to trim the edges after stitching the layers of your quilt. Trimming will make sure that your quilt hangs straight when displayed on a wall.

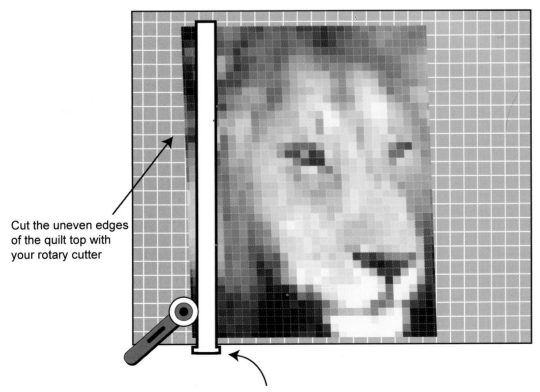

Cut the uneven edges of the quilt top with your rotary cutter

Slide the lip of the ruler along the edge of the mat to cut stright lines.

## Adding Borders

A border is a straight strip of fabric sewn around the edges of your quilt to finish it.

A border can make your photo quilt even more beautiful but borders also have a practical purpose. Adding a border will make the edges of the quilt perfectly straight, and the corners will be perfectly squared. The border will make the quilted photo hang perfectly straight on the wall without any wavy edges. Another added bonus is the border will increase the size of the quilt and provide a place to put decorative quilting.

Adding a border is a decision you will make after you see the finished quilt top. You can add one or two borders or have no border at all.

When you think about adding borders to your quilted photos, you can pretend you are adding a matting and frame. Pay attention to the way paper

photographs are framed. Also look at how paintings and other works of art are finished. Notice how the colors relate to the art work, and pay close attention to the proportion of the border in relation to the art work.

There are two types of borders, straight cut borders and mitered borders. I will explain both types.

To add a border, the first step is to measure at the center of the quilt in both directions. You can see an example of this on the next page. Be sure to measure in the center of the quilt because the edges of the quilt are probably stretched and are not accurate. The center measurements will determine what length to cut the border strips. Cut the borders strips across the width of the fabric.

Diagram A - Straight Border

Diagram B - Mitered Border

### Straight border

A straight border has straight seams on the corners. See diagram A on page 46. To add a

2. Cut two border strips the the exact cemter measurement for the top and bottom. Stitch the border pieces to the quilt top with a 1/4" seam allowance. Ease the quilt top to the border if it is necessary.

3. Measure the quilt and the border in the vertically

Measure the in the center

4. Cut two border strips the the exact vertical measurement for each side of the quilt. Stitch the border pieces to the quilt top with a 1/4" seam allowance. Ease the quilt top to the border if it is necessary.

straight border, the first step is to measure the center of the quilt horizontally. Cut two border strips this exact length. Stitch the borders to the sides of the quilt, easing the quilt top to match the border if it is necessary.

Next measure the center of the quilt in the vertical direction including the border that you just applied. Cut two border strips that exact length. Stitch the border to the quilt, easing the two together if it is necessary. If you want a second straight border, repeat this process.

### Mitered border

A mitered border is a border with diagonal seam on the corners. See

diagram B on page 46.

To add a mitered border, first measure the center of the quilt in the vertical direction. Next measure the width of the border. Now cut two border strips the vertical length + the width of the border times 2. Mark the width of the border on each end of the border pieces. Cut the corners as shown in the diagram below. Cut from the outside corner, down to the border marks. Stitch the border pieces to the sides of the quilt, easing the quilt into the border if it is necessary. Stop your stitching 1/4" from the edge. Repeat these steps for the horizontal edges of the quilt top.

### To Create The Corner Seams

Fold the quilt in half diagonally so that the ends of the border meet. Stitch the corner seams with 1/4" seam allowances. Repeat this step for all four corners. You can see a diagram of how to create a corner on the next page.

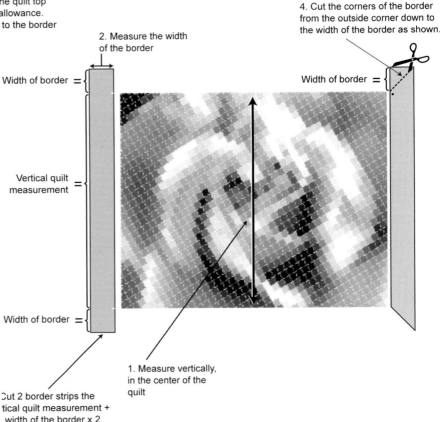

2. Measure the width of the border

4. Cut the corners of the border from the outside corner down to the width of the border as shown.

Width of border =

Width of border =

Vertical quilt measurement =

Width of border =

1. Measure vertically, in the center of the quilt

Cut 2 border strips the tical quilt measurement + width of the border x 2

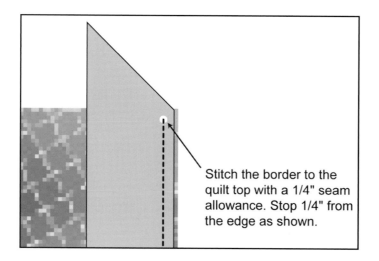

Stitch the border to the quilt top with a 1/4" seam allowance. Stop 1/4" from the edge as shown.

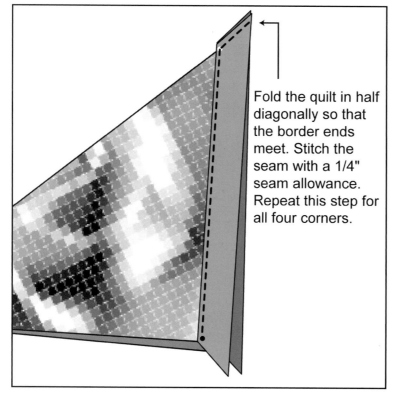

Fold the quilt in half diagonally so that the border ends meet. Stitch the seam with a 1/4" seam allowance. Repeat this step for all four corners.

## Batting and Backing

You can choose any backing fabric because the back of the quilt does not show. However I always use one of the fabrics that were used on the front of the quilt.

If your quilt top is larger than the width of the backing fabric, you will have to stitch two pieces of the backing fabric together to cover the back of the quilt. Remember to iron the backing seam open if a seam is required for your backing.

To sign your quilt, you can sign directly on the backing with a permanent pigment ink pen if you use a light colored fabric, or you can create an embroidered signature. You can also choose to apply a label to the back of the quilt.

The batting you use between the quilt top and the backing is again a matter of your preference. Batting is sold in standard bedding sizes as well as by the yard. Cotton battings are flatter when they are finished than polyester battings, but polyester and cotton blends are a good option as well. I usually use 100% cotton batting for my quilted photos. You can find batting in fabric and quilt stores.

For a textured quilt, you might decide to not have batting at all. The multiple layers of fabric make the quilt kind of heavy but I like to add batting because it gives the quilt structure and helps is stay square and flat.

### Basting

Basting is a temporary bond that holds the quilt top, batting and backing together. Basting also assures that you will not have tucks or folds on the backing when you stich through your quilt sandwich.

You can baste the quilt sandwich by hand with a running stitch as shown in example A on the next page

My favorite way to baste is to use an adhesive basting spray. It is easy to find in chain and quilt stores. Spray the adhesive between each layer of the quilt and the layers will hold together for the quilting process.

## Bindings

After the quilting is finished, you still need to finish the edges. You will finish the edges with a binding and I will show you how to make two different types.

Basting stitched through the quilt sandwich

Quilt Top

Backing

Batting

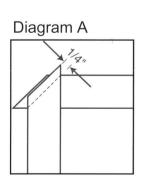

Example A

Fold the binding strip in half the long way, and then place the binding on the front of the quilt with the raw edges together. Stitch the binding with a ¼" seam allowance as shown in diagram B.

### Diagram B

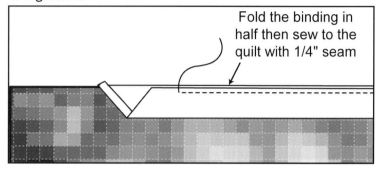

Fold the binding in half then sew to the quilt with 1/4" seam

To continue the binding around the corner, stop stitching ¼" from the edge.

### Diagram C

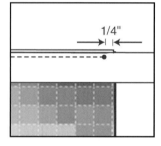

1/4"

Fold the binding upward, creating an angled corner as shown in diagram D.

### Diagram D

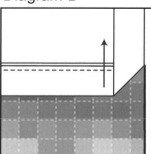

The first type of binding is a classic binding and the second type is an invisible binding.

## Classic Binding

A classic binding will make a ¼" edge around the outside of the quilt. To make a classic binding, the first thing you will do is cut strips 1½" wide. Cut the strips across the width of the fabric. Stitch the strips together to form one long strip as shown in diagram A.

### Diagram A

1/4"

Then fold the binding back downward (creating a squared corner), leaving a fold of fabric as shown. Pin the fold in place and stitch the next side of the binding. You can begin stitching from the corner edge.

## Diagram E

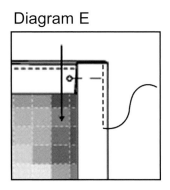

The next step is to wrap the binding around the quilt edge, then over to the back as shown in diagram F. The last step is to stitch the edge of the binding in place with a small whipstitch.

## Diagram F

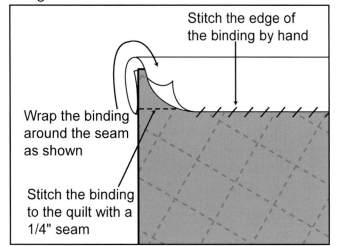

Stitch the edge of the binding by hand

Wrap the binding around the seam as shown

Stitch the binding to the quilt with a 1/4" seam

### Invisible Binding

An invisible binding will not show at all when viewing the quilt from the front. To make an invisible binding, the first thing you will do is cut strips 1½" wide. Fold the binding strip in half, and then place the binding on the front of the quilt with the raw edges together. Stitch the binding with a ¼" seam allowance as shown in diagram B on page 49.

After stitching the binding all the way around the quilt, fold the binding and the seam upward, and away from the quilt. Stitch the binding 1/8" away from the seam as shown in the diagram below. This stitch will force the binding and the seam allowance to roll towards the backside of the quilt.

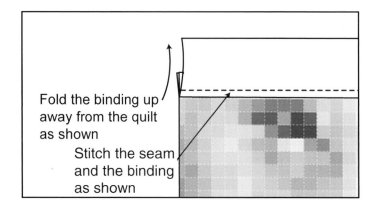

Fold the binding up away from the quilt as shown

Stitch the seam and the binding as shown

The last step is to stitch the edge of the binding in place with a small whipstitch.

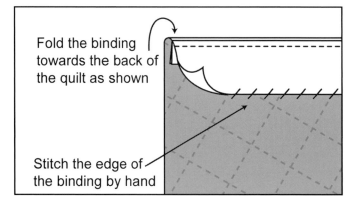

Fold the binding towards the back of the quilt as shown

Stitch the edge of the binding by hand

## How to display a Quilted Photo

When you prepare to display your quilt, you first need to think about how to care for the quilt. The most important thing you can do to preserve the quilt is to use UV protection spray if your quilt will be exposed to sun light. This spray will act just like a sunscreen and protect the fabrics from fading.

Since these quilts are intended to be art that is hung on a wall, you should not have to worry about the quilts getting dirty. However you will need to remove dust from time to time if they are not framed behind glass. To remove the dust, just put the quilt in a clothes dryer for 10 minutes. The dryer will remove the dust without damaging the quilt.

After you have learned how to care for your quilt, you must decide how you will display it. The most obvious way to display your quilt is to have it framed professionally.

Another way you can display the quilt is to stretch it over a blank canvas. If you want to stretch it on a canvas you will not need to add a backing, batting or a binding. Center it over the canvas, then use a staple gun to secure the quilt top to the wooden frame of the canvas.

The way that I prefer to display my quilts is to add a sleeve to the back of the quilt as shown in the diagram below. To add a sleeve, just make a 4" fabric tube the width of the quilt, then hand stitch it to the top of the quilt on both sides of the tube. To hang the quilt you will need a cafe curtain rod. Apply the curtain rod to the wall according to the manufacturer's instructions. Pull the curtain rod through the sleeve to hang the quilt. You can buy cafe curtain rods at any hardware store.

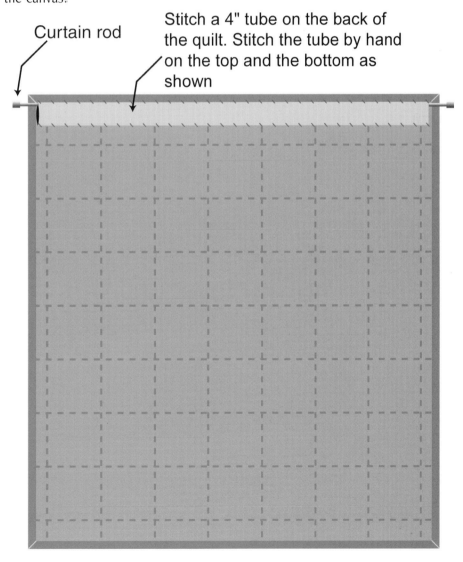

Curtain rod

Stitch a 4" tube on the back of the quilt. Stitch the tube by hand on the top and the bottom as shown

**Customer Photos**

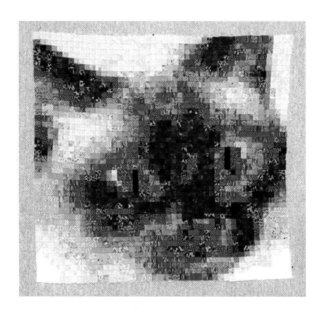

# How To Make Your Own Patterns With QPX 1.0

## In this chapter

- How to download the software
- System requirements
- Program tools
- Using the program tools
- Finding the values of your fabrics

## How To Download The Software

To download the software you must have internet access. Go to this address:
www.quiltedphoto.com/indexfree.html
To get the software, enter
this access code: **96985314**

## System Requirements

1. Microsoft Windows 95 or later
2. 90 MHz processor
3. 16 MB RAM
4. 32-bit color is a system requirement
5. A way to get photos into your computer(Photo processing CD, Scanner, digital camera, etc.)

If the Processed Photo does not display correctly within the program window, your display settings are set to either 16 or 256 colors. For the program to work properly, you must be able to display 32bit true color or greater. This is how to change your display settings: click Start->Control Panel, then
double-click Display->Settings. Under "Colors," you need to select 32bit true color or greater.

### Installation
1. Double click file: "Setup.exe".
2. Follow the installer's on-screen instructions.

## Program Tools

**A. Original Photo Display**
This is the display of the original Photograph

**B. Processed Photograph.**
The processed photo changes as you change the settings below.

**C. Detail Slider Bar.**
As you move the selector, you will dynamically see the processed photo change.

**D. Photo Detail Information Box**
See how many pieces your quilt will have with the the current photo detail slider bar settings.

**E. Number Of Fabrics selector Bar.**
Slide the bar to the right to increase the number of fabrics or to the left to decrease. You will be able to dynamically see how the number of fabrics change the processed photo.

**F. Number Of Fabrics Information Box.** This displays the number of fabrics with the the current number of fabrics slider bar setting.

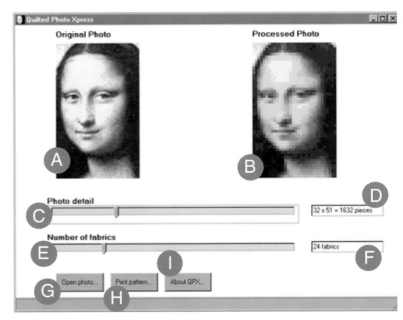

### G. Open Photo Button

Click this button to choose your own photos. You can use the following image formats: Bmp, jpeg and wmf

### H. Print Pattern

Click this button to print your quilted photo pattern.

### I. About QPX

Click this button for information about Mosaic Quilt Studio, and the software.

### J. Selection Tool

You can also select a smaller area of your photo with the selection tool. You can use it by putting you cursor over your original photograph and holding down your left mouse button. Drag the mouse until the area you want as you pattern is selected. Let go of the left mouse button and process the photo with the other tools. When you select an area of the photo a button called "Restore" will appear. This button will restore the photo back to normal.

Original Photo

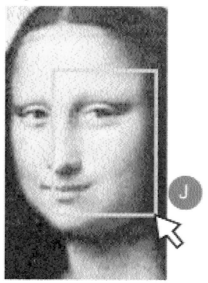

Click and drag to zoom in

## Using The Program Tools

### How Many Fabric Squares

The answer to this question depends on how much detail is in the image. If the image has a lot of small details then you will have to use more fabric squares to see the details clearly. If you decide to use to few squares, the image will look blurry. For a close-up image of a face, 1000 to 1600 squares is enough to see the image clearly, but for a dollar bill or a building, the small details may dictate 3000 -4000 pieces.

Photograph with lots of small details

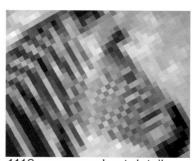

1112 squares = Lost details

3424 squares = Clear details

## Straight Or Angled Grid

Your choice about what grid to use is just a matter of what you like most. The straight grid and the angled grid work equally well. If you want to make a photo with an angled grid you will need to turn the photo on and angle with a photo editing software or you can simply turn the photo on an angle when you scan it into your computer.

Making a pattern on the angle is not required for any of the techniques in this book but it can make your quilted photo more interesting. If you want to turn your photo on an angle, my suggestion is that you place the photo on a very dark or a white sheet of paper while scanning. This is so that you can tell which squares of the pattern are the background and not include them in your quilt.

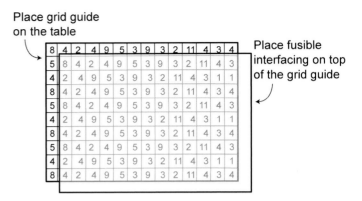

Place grid guide on the table

Place fusible interfacing on top of the grid guide

If the pattern has a straight grid then put the guide under the interfacing the same way it appears. If you made your pattern on an angle then use the following instructions for positioning the grid guide.

You will need a quilting ruler that has a 30 degree or a 60 degree mark on it. Line up the 30 or 60 degree angle with the straight edge of the interfacing as shown in the diagram A. Mark a 30 degree line as shown in the

Straight Grid

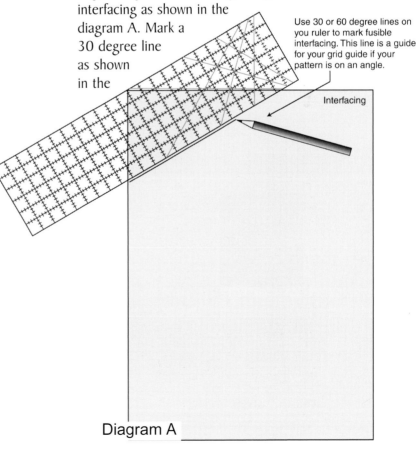

Use 30 or 60 degree lines on you ruler to mark fusible interfacing. This line is a guide for your grid guide if your pattern is on an angle.

Interfacing

Diagram A

Angled Grid

diagram.

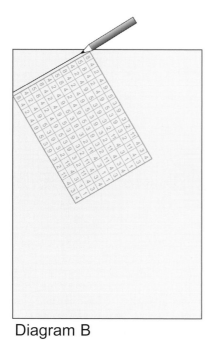

Diagram B

Next you will line up the edge of the grid with the angled line you have drawn(diagram B).

If you made your pattern on an angle other than

## Determine Values With Software

30 or 60 degree, then match the angle of your pattern for this step.

I discussed finding the values of your fabrics and taught you how to use a photocopy machine to see the values in chapter 2, but using the software is another way to do it. Cut a 1", square piece of the fabrics to make your quilted photo. (remember the 888 rule in chapter 2).Your goal is to have colored fabrics that represent shades from light to dark.

Place the squares on the form at the end of this chapter. Please cut the squares exactly 1" so that the entire width of the page is covered by fabric. If your fabric pieces are smaller than 1", the white spaces between the squares will make your results confusing.It is also important to make all of your fabrics fit on the page at one time.

Scan your form into your computer and save the image of your fabrics as a jpeg file. Open your file

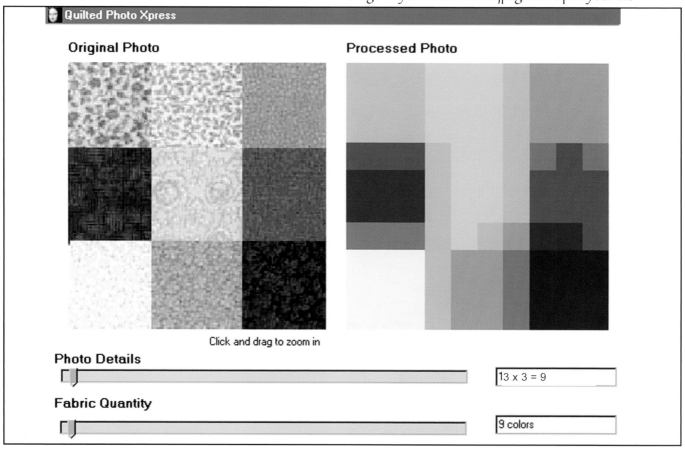

in the Quilted Photo Xpress 1.0 Original Photo Display window. Now move the Number Of Fabrics selector Bar to match the number of fabrics on your form.
Next move the Photo Detail Slider all the way to the left, until the number it says matches the fabrics across the top row.

Use the selection tool to only select the fabrics, and none of the surrounding form as shown in the diagram. This part is tricky so try until your selection is perfect.

The last thing to do is print the pattern. You will ignore everything except the grid of numbers. The grid will tell you what value each of the swatches are. The pattern will look something like the diagram below.

If two of your swatches have the same color value, then make your decision by looking at the fabrics to determine the value, or choose another fabric and start the process over again.

If you want to make life easier, consider using the 'Valuations' software to sort your fabrics. With 'Valuations' the sorting process is automatic. You can get more details about 'Valuations" on page 69.

| 3 | 2 | 5 |
|---|---|---|
| 7 | 2 | 5 |
| 1 | 4 | 9 |

## Quilted Photo Xpress /Color Value Swatch Form

| | | | | |
|---|---|---|---|---|
| Attach Fabric Swatch Here | Attach Fabric Swatch Here | Attach Fabric Swatch Here | Attach Fabric Swatch Here | Attach Fabric Swatch Here |
| Attach Fabric Swatch Here | Attach Fabric Swatch Here | Attach Fabric Swatch Here | Attach Fabric Swatch Here | Attach Fabric Swatch Here |
| Attach Fabric Swatch Here | Attach Fabric Swatch Here | Attach Fabric Swatch Here | Attach Fabric Swatch Here | Attach Fabric Swatch Here |

# Conclusion

For this third book, my goal was to combine quilted photography and texture. It has been a exciting and challenging journey. The more I worked on the quilts, the more new ideas I seemed to get.Now that the book is finished, I am proud of the practical techniques I have included in the book. I really hope you like them too.

I have a new email newsletter ! I have not sent much email in the last couple of years but I plan to share more ideas with you every month. I will also show you my latest quilts many new tips and quilts from other quilters who also love Quilted Photography. Go to my website to get your free email subscription. You will find the sign up page as soon as you go to: www.QuiltedPhoto.com

You should go to my website NOW to download your free version of Quilted Photo Xpress 1.0. 'Quilted Photo Xpress 1.0' software will make a quilting pattern out of any photo. It prints patterns in grayscale only and the patterns are used with grid guides.You can download the software at: www.QuiltedPhoto.com/indexfree.html
The password is:  96985314

Did you know that you can get free grid guides. I have included coupons in the catalog that entitle you to one of each of the grid guides described in this book. The calalog starts on page 69 and the free coupon is on page 75.

I have enjoyed sharing my techniques, and my quilts with you. I would like to see your Quilted Photos too! I don't get to see enough of your quilts! Please send me pictures of your projects, I might include you in my next book.

email: tammie@mosaicquilt.com
or
Mosaic Quilt Studio
917 Fremont Ave PMB138
South Pasadena, CA 91030

Thank you for your continued interest in "Quilted Photography"!

**Tammie Bowser**

# Special Thanks

Thank you Zoza for the beautiful tulip photograph in chapter 5. Zoza has more incredible photographs available and I really think you should see them. Go to **www.ZozaShots.net** phone 310-486-2108

Thank you to JD Stencils for sharing your wonderful stencils with me.
**www.jdstencils.com**

Thank you to Starr Designs at **www.starrfabrics.com** and The Chicken Tree **www.thechickentree.com** for sharing your lovely fabrics with me.

Thank you once again to Janome America for the fantastic sewing machines! The Memorycraft 11000 and the beautiful 6500. These machines have made my work more creative and enjoyable. I highly recommend that you try out these machines if you are considering a new sewing machine!
**www.Janome.com**

Special Thanks to Sue Ann Taylor and Quilters News Network for having me as a guest on your show and making me a quilting star all over the world! QNN has 24 hour a day quilt programming from your computer! To see my shows and lots of others, go to **www.QuiltersNewsNetwork.com**

I began sewing at four years of age. With my natural talent for sewing I made my own clothing in jr. high and high school. I went on to fashion college (The Fashion Institute of Design and Merchandising). I studied fashion design, color theory and pattern making then graduated in 1985. My 17 year fashion career included positions as a fashion designer, production patternmaker and first patternmaker.

I also studied website design, graphic design and desktop publishing. My new computer knowledge combined perfectly with my design, fashion, and sewing knowledge. I went on to start a website called www.Ez-fit.com. This site makes custom sized clothing patterns for people who sew.

Throughout my busy careers, I held an interest in quilting but, never took the time to learn it. With lots of time at home after My daughter was born, in the fall of 2000, I began to read books about quilting. Quilting captivated me, and I began to focus my creativity towards it.

Tammie & daughter Angela

I made my first quilt as a gift for my mother in November of 2000. I taught myself how to quilt by reading books, and watching the HGTV series, "Simply Quilts". After making that first quilt, I wanted to design my own quilt patterns. One morning just a few weeks later, I woke up with the idea for Quilted Photos. My first thought was that it couldn't work, but I made the first quilted photo that very week. I was amazed at how stunning the results were, and am still amazed every time I complete a Quilted Photo.

I think my career paths, and collection of knowledge has given me this unique approach to quilting. I hope you enjoy this innovative quilting style as much as I do.

Look for Tammie on HGTV's "Simply Quilts" episode #819, Kaye Wood's show "Friends of Kaye" #K1404 and "Sewing with Nancy" on PBS.

## Customer Quilts

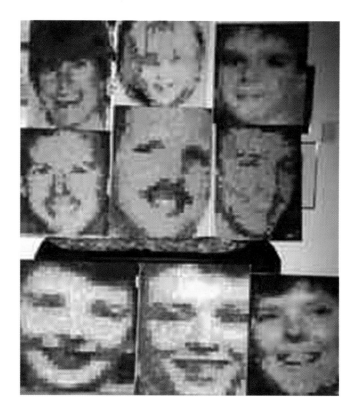

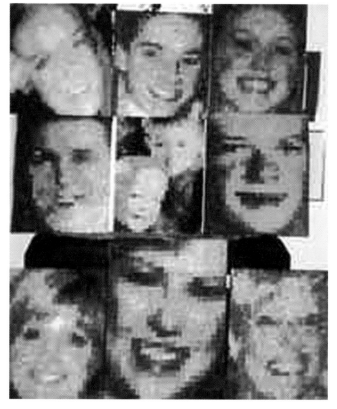

Tammie,

I'm so very proud of the quilt below. It's of my father (who passed away last year) and I'm giving it to my mom for Mother's Day. You helped me out with a couple of the colors through e-mail. Everyone has seen it has been absolutely stunned that this looks just like him! Your program is unbelievable. I love the color palette, which was a great help in choosing just the right fabrics. This quilt has 3060 pieces in 24 colors. I did it in the one-inch squares. Although it took me a long time to sew as the squares were so small, it was completely worth it. I took it to my local fabric stores to look for binding and backing and it was a hit! One of the employees took it around showing it to everyone. I was in Jo-Ann Fabrics for over an hour talking to people about it. They were in awe. I can't wait to start my next one!

Sincerely,
Cindi Allen

Thank you for sending me the number grid and extra tricot fusible so promptly. (I was in your class in Lansing, MI) I stayed up until 3AM working on the quilt. Last night I finally finished it and at first, thought it didn't work. Then I tacked it on the wall and backed up and just said, "Oh my gosh" I couldn't believe it turned out. What fun! I can hardly wait to show it off at show and tell at my ASG meeting. Thank you for creating such a delightful technique. I have printed out the grid for a photo of my granddaughter in blacks and whites with the software. Now to find enough fabric for it. Thank you again.
Nancy Kiernan

Hi, I'd like to tell you how glad I am that I saw you on Simply Quilts. I was so impressed and immediately had the idea to make a Mosaic Quilt of my daughter and her son. I enjoyed the process so much, it was also a healing process for me because the baby in the picture, Andrew, my grandson, passed away in June, 2004 at the age of 2. It was very emotional when I gave the quilt to my daughter and her family. I'd like to share with you a picture of it. Thank you so much for sharing your technique.
Karen Thompson

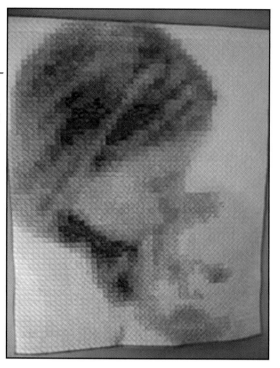

p.s. I just love it hanging in my family room. I think I forgot to mention that I made two of the same exact quilts so that I could have one too.

Tammie,
I am really happy with this. The dog's name is Ivy. Everyone who has seen it just can't believe how easy it was to do. I can't wait to do more!!
Joyce Dunn

Tammie, I thought you would like to see the first quilted photo that I did of my sister for her birthday. I am not a quilter, but I enjoyed the software. I learned a lot from this first one. I plan to do one of my two dogs--Lhasa Apsos--next and since one is black and one is white, I feel it will be quite a challenge.

Jeanie Wallace

Picture of mosaic quilt we did for our church!
Everyone loves it. Thanks to you. Fran

Hi Tammie,
I wanted to share my first quilt with you. I have been thinking about making a quilt for several years, but didn't feel I had the time. When I saw you on Sewing with Nancy, I immediately looked for your website as I knew that this process would be relatively quick. I loved pressing the pieces on and see-ing the pattern come to life. Thanks for your software and your quilting process. I have attached both my quilt and the photo I used for the pattern.

Regards,
Shari Sands

Thanks for the quick response. Attached is the original photo and a picture of the quilt about half way done. I think it is looking pretty good. I finished laying out the squares and have been sewing it together. I ran out of bobbin thread twice already. I guess it takes a lot of thread! I will send you another picture when I get it done. Murphy Quilt is a painting my sister did of her dog that just passed away. Murphy2 is the photoquilt 1/2 layed out.

Ginny Patterson

Tammie, I just completed my first quilt!!!!!! and I am so excited about it. This weekend I will be starting my second one (my three grandson). I have to admit with the first one, I really thought I made mistakes especially with the light colors. I chose a light green and it kinda stands out. But the photo is beautiful. I've ordered the pre-arranged fabrics from Nancy and look forward to using Batiks I truly believe that they will be better. I will send you copies of both quilts when completed....I have to use the computers at the library and on the job to download the more amazing quilt disc....I know now that I will have to invest in a new computer with scanning and photo printing capabilities....MAY GOD CONTINUE TO BLESS AND PLEASE KEEP ME ON YOUR MAILING LIST FOR UPCOMMING SEQUALS TO MORE AMAZINGING QUILT PHOTOGRAPHY.....
Gwen. Cooper

Thank you so much. I am almost finished with my first quilt!! It is of my grandson and the results so far are incredible. I followed your instructions and arranged the fabrics according to value. From then I had to go on faith because some of the fabrics looked the same to me.

Up until now, quilting had never appealed to me. It made no sense to me to cut up little pieces of good fabric just to sew them together again. But this is totally different. This is art.
Thanks for sharing your knowledge.
Sincerely,
Victoria Bledsoe

Tammie,
I wanted to let you know that every time we offer your book as a class at Hartsdale Fabrics, we have an enthusiastic turnout, and the students have done some amazing quilts using your method. I am attaching a photo I just received from one of my students, this was a rather large and ambitious project she did of her family skiing. I thought you would enjoy seeing it.
Leni Wiener

"Dear Tammie, I lost my son in 1992 and have been seeking a new way to keep him near even more than I already do with his photographs. Your wonderful gift has given me something very precious that I can share with other family members. I'll be making one for my daughter too. This is such a precious gift! Thank you for sharing your great ideas. You must be a wonderful mother, as just listening to you speak about your daughter brings that feeling of warmth and tenderness. May God bless you in your life and family."
Carolyn Snell

Here is the complete picture with the boxer. It has 5475 pieces and won an award in a San Diego quilt show!

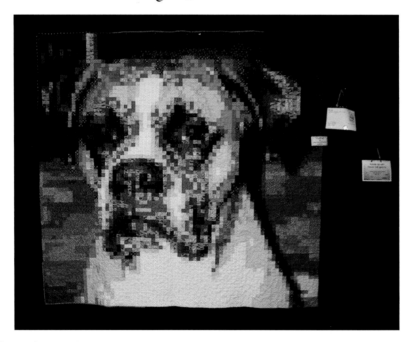

Hi Tammie..
I just wanted to let you know how much fun I had making my 1st mosaic quilt. I got the pattern ready, all the material cut & attached in 1 weekend.  Then I did the quilting part off and on this week after work. I'm attaching a copy of the quilt for you to see.  I really like it and had such a good time....  Even my husband was having a good time watching it come to life! Thank you!
Diana Miller

## What's In this catalog

- ◆ Software
- ◆ Notions / Supplies
- ◆ Fabric
- ◆ Books
- ◆ Coupons

### new **Valuations Software**

Valuations is new and it will sort your fabrics instantly! The software is easy to use and when you press the "Sort Fabrics" button.....the fabrics switch around to the correct order by color value! This will even work with hundreds of fabrics! Why not sort your whole fabric collection! It's easy, it's fast, and it never fails. No nore guessing! Perfect for 'Quilted Photography' or any other project that requires sorting your fabrics by color value!

## PC / Mac $39.95

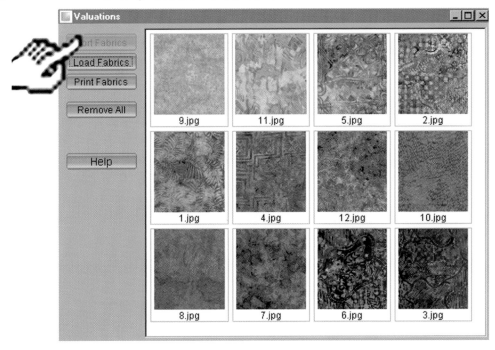

## new **Quilted Photo Xpress 3.0**

Completely new software design! This new version of Quilted Photo Xpress has been made even better!

**Grid Angle**
- ⦿ Straight
- ○ 30 Degree Angle
- ○ 45 Degree Angle

To start with, at the click of a button you can change the angle of the pattern. If you want your Quilted Photo Quilt to be turned on point, just click the button and wait a few seconds for the preview! In the screen shot below I selected 30 degree angle. You should also pay attention to the new Chenille Rag options!

☐ 1 ¼" Chenilled Rag
☐ 1 ½" Chenilled Rag

This option will automatically make patterns for the technique in chapter 6, no need for Grid Guides if you have QPX3!

Another completely new feature is the ability to print your own fabric directly from your printer!!! Shall I say that again? Print your fabrics directly from

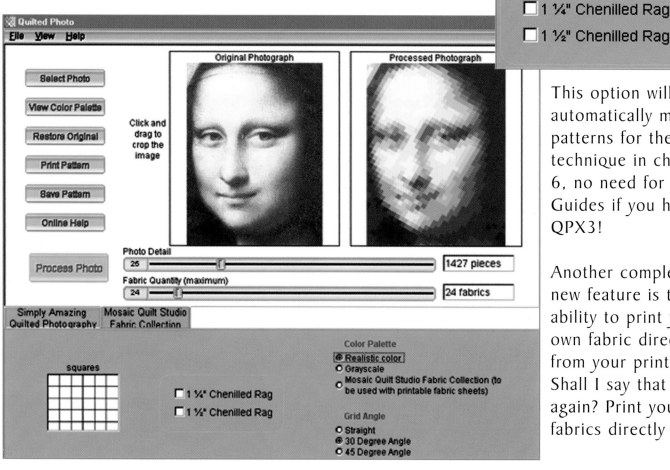

your inkjet printer with printable fabric sheets! QPX3 will calculate the correct amount of each fabric and all the colors you will need...then just feed your printer with printable fabric sheets.....how can it be any easier? It can't!

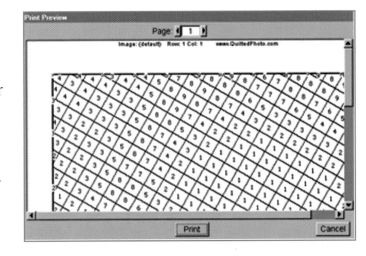

I listened to the user of the previous versions of Quilted Photo Xpress and I have added features that you asked for:

1. Added a new Preview Window. Now you can see a preview of your patterns before they are printed!

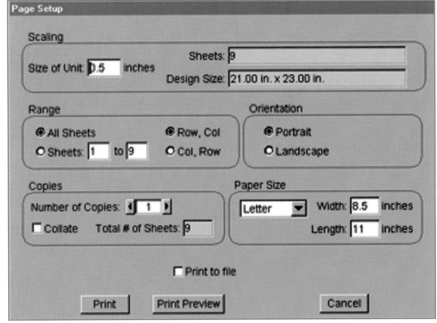

2. You also have the ability to choose the size of your finished quilt percisely, with the all new print setup window. You can also see just how many pages your pattern will be.......in other words you have complete control over your patterns.

3. The numbers are bigger and easy to see! It is a simple change but a very useful change!

4. The palette preview window and printout is bigger and have larger swatches to help you choose your fabrics!

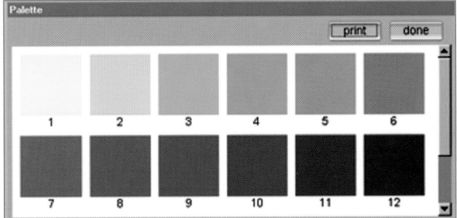

Quilted Photo Xpress 3.0 is now available in Mac version too!

Upgrades are available for Paid users of Quilted Photo Xpress 1.0 and 2.0, Upgrade is not available for users of free software. See page 79 for details. **PC / Mac $79.95**

## Grid Guides

The Grid Guide is an essential too for making a Quilted Photo if you are using the free software. It is a printed grid that is used along with fusible interfacing to position the fabric squares in the correct order. Tape them together to
form a bigger grid with less erasing. Three sizes are available.

## Packaged 4 for $10.00

## Quilt Basting Spray

Stick your fabric layers together instantly with this spray! It is a repositionable, temporary bond that will hold strong until you wash it out with water. It washes out completely, and it is orderless and colorless. The spray will not gum your sewing machine needle.

## $13.00 per can

## Water-Soluble Wonder Tape

This water-soluble tape completely disappears in the first washing. Double sided transparent tape that can be stitched through and will not gum up the needle. It is 1/4" wide and 360 inches long, Use it with the water-soluble stabilizer to make quilted photos with texture.

## $3.70 per roll

## Water-Soluble Stabilizer

This stabilizer is completely clear so that you can see your pattern numbers right through it! This stabilizer is used for every textured tecnique in this book! It washes away completely with water. Use it with Wonder Tape. It is 40" wide and is sold by the yard.

## $3.00 per yard

## Free Lace Sticky Stabilizer

This stabilizer is used the same way as the stabilizer above except you don't need the Wonder Tape because it is already sticky on one side. It is an easy to use and works great.
It is 28 1/2" wide.

## $19.30 per yard

## Fabric Packs

Finally let Tammie select your fabrics for you! She has hand dyed cotton fabrics available in three color ways. Black & White, Sepia and Multi-Color. They are beautiful and you don't have to agonize about your fabric selections!

The Black & White and Sepia will create old fashioned looking images, just like your old photographs! They come with 12 fabrics each, in order from light to dark and already number for you to start making your quilt as soon as your fabrics arrive.
Each of the 12 fabrics is 1/4 yard

### $45 each

The Multi Color assortment of fabrics are just beautiful! They are hand-dyed by Hoffman in an assortment that is full of color. This assortment has 24 fabrics in order from light to dark and already numbered for you. Each of the 24 fabrics is 1/8th yard.

### $50 each

## -Simply Amazing Quilted Photography

Make a quilted photograph in just a weekend with only 24 fabrics! Tammie's book features 10 patterns to get you started, and urges you to try out her technique to make your own photos into quilts. She teaches you how to choose a photo, color palettes and her 8-8-8 rule. This amazing technique is a great way to transform a snapshot into a family heirloom or a quick easy gift.
**$24.95**

## -More Amazing Quilted Photography

The popular book "Simply Amazing Quilted Photography" has an amazing sequel! "More Amazing Quilted Photography" Learn to translate photos into quilted fabric art. You can use the techniques Tammie uses to win quilt show ribbons! Includes 4 exciting new techniques and variations, 2 new ways to quilt your quilted photos, easy ways to choose your fabric colors and learn a foolproof way to easily put your fabrics in order from light to dark. **$29.95**

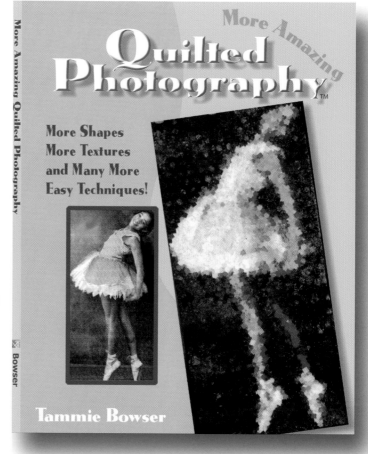

# Quilted Photography Coupons

Coupons

"I recently finished a photo quilt of my granddaughter and it is amazing to say the least.
Everyone gasps when they see it and I can hardly wait to have it in our guild's quilt show in July. Thank you for this lovely technique. I will send you a photo of it as soon as I finish quilting it."
**Yvonne Moore**

"These quilts are extremely easy and fun to make! They make great gift quilts. The instructions are easy to follow and your class was a lot of fun! This is a great quilt for any beginner or advanced quilter!"
**Sue Vite**

"The quilt I made in class has won First Place in two shows, one Judges Choice and one Best of Show!"
**Marlene Pearson**
**Santa Barbara, CA**

"My Daughter Rosie (14 years old), made a Quilted Photo of a dolphin and entered it in the Los Angeles County Fair. She won a BLUE RIBBON and is very proud of her quilt! Thank You"
**Katherine R.**
**Pasadena, CA**

# Quilted Photography Coupons

## $8.00 off Fabric Packs

Do you want me to pick your fabrics for you? Well I have! With this coupon you can buy one Black & White or Sepia fabric pack for only $37. Check one box below.

☐ Send me one fabric pack with Black & White cotton fabrics. Twelve values,1/8th yard pieces

OR

☐ Send me one fabric pack with Sepia cotton fabrics. Twelve values, 1/8th yard pieces

**Quilted Photography Coupon # AC104**

$4 Value

## Ruler Guide
### only $1.00 w/ any purchase

**Quilted Photography Coupon # AC105**

$4 Value

## Small Ruler Handle
### only $1.00 w/ any purchase

**Quilted Photography Coupon # AC106**

## $10.00 off the price of 'Quilted Photography' books

Do you have all if the Quilted Photography books? Well if you don't this is the time to get them! This coupon will take $10 off the price of each book & you can get up to 3 books with this coupon......Why not buy them for gifts! Fill out the form below

Save up to $30

| Qty | | Unit Price | Sub - Total |
|---|---|---|---|
| | 'Simply Amazing Quilted Photography' | $14.95 | |
| | 'More Amazing Quilted Photography' | $19.95 | |
| | 'Amazing Chenilled Quilted Photography' | $19.95 | |
| | Enter Grand Total On Order Form | | |

**Quilted Photography Coupon # AC107**

# Order Form

"I love this technique! Simple to sew and so rewarding!"
**Marlene P.**
**Santa Barbara, CA**

"Your class was the best I have attended! Everyone placing squares of fabric, critiquing colors, pressing and sewing. Then the oooohs and aaaahs; as masterpieces appeared, as if by magic. Everyone who has seen the Quilted Photo of my grandchild cannot believe it was possible to achieve! When they cannot figure it out, they look across the room at the mirror opposite of it and GASP. Thank you Tammie for a great innovative creation."
**Carolyn V.**
**Sierra Madre, CA**

"I loved your Quilted PhotoTM  class. It is such a great sewing idea, as well as easy. I loved it and so did my family. I gave my mom the quilt for mother's day and she loved it. Your quilt idea helped me enjoy sewing and it is my motivation to continue to learn more techniques and ideas. Thank You"
Nicole C.
Los Angeles, CA

# Useful Items For Other 'Quilted Photography' Techniques

| Description | Unit Price | Qty. | Subtotal |
|---|---|---|---|
| Quilted Photo Xpress 3.0 Upgrade (from 1.0) | $40.00 | | |
| Quilted Photo Xpress 3.0 Upgrade (from 2.0) | $25.00 | | |
| Steam-A-Seam2 18" wide (per yard) | $6.75 | | |
| Large Ruler Handle | $5.00 | | |
| Silicone Spray | $7.95 | | |
| Ruler Guide | $4.00 | | |
| Extra Wide Fusible Tricot (per yard) | $6.10 | | |
| Extra Wide Web (per yard) | $4.90 | | |
| UV Protection Spray | $13.95 | | |
| Fabric Organizer Box | $12.80 | | |
| Distance Viewer | $7.95 | | |
| Non-Stitck Pressign Sheet (per yard) | $9.50 | | |

**Note:** To upgrade the Quilted Photo software, you must include the paper cover of the software you have with your order as proof of purchase.

**Grand Total**

**Turn the page over and transfer total to complete the order form**

Order Form

# Get Amazing Chenilled Quilted Photography Supplies!

## Order Form

**Postal Orders:**
Mosaic Quilt Studio
917 Fremont, PMB138
South Pasadena, CA 91030, USA

**Fax Orders:**
(626)799-5998 (do not fax coupons)

**Telephone Orders:**
1-800-290-6705 or (626)799-5998
Have your AMEX,
Mastercard or Visa ready

## FREE SHIPPING (US only)
## on all orders over $100

Shipping Charges

| | |
|---|---|
| $25.00 and under | $7.50 |
| $25.01 to $49.99 | $10.00 |
| $50.00 and $99.99 | 14.00 |
| $100.00 and over | FREE |

International Shipping charges will vary by location

## Payment Method

☐ **Mastercard**
☐ **Visa**
☐ **American Express**
☐ **Check / Money Order**

### Do you want my email Newsletter?

I have a new email newsletter ! I will share more ideas with you every month. I will also show you my latest quilts and photos from other quilters who love Quilted Photography and many new tips. Fill in your email address to start your free subscription.

| Description | Unit Price | Qty. | Subtotal |
|---|---|---|---|
| Valuations 1.0 Software | $39.95 | | |
| Quilted Photo Xpress 3.0 Software (Full Version) | $79.95 | | |
| Grid Guide 4 Pack (11/4" and 11/2") | $10.00 | | |
| Grid Guide 4 Pack (3/4" and 1") | $10.00 | | |
| Grid Guide 4 Pack (Chenille) | $10.00 | | |
| Free-Lace Sticky Stabilizer by the yard (28.5" wide) | $19.30 | | |
| Quilt Basting Spray | $13.00 | | |
| Water-Soluble Stabilizer by the yard (40" wide) | $3.00 | | |
| Water-Soluble Double Stick Tape (per roll) | $3.70 | | |
| Cotton Fabric Pack- Black & White (12 quarter yd. pieces) | $45.00 | | |
| Cotton Fabric Pack- Sepia (12 quarter yd. pieces) | $45.00 | | |
| Cotton Fabric Pack - Multi Color (24 eighth yd. pieces) | $50.00 | | |
| Simply Amazing Quilted Photography | $24.95 | | |
| More Amazing Quilted Photography | $29.95 | | |
| Amazing Chenilled Quilted Photography | $29.95 | | |

**Original coupon must be included with order - Limit 2 coupons per order**

| | | |
|---|---|---|
| Coupon # | | |
| Coupon # | | |
| Sub-Total from other side of page | | |
| Total Item Price | | |
| CA residents include 8.25% sales tax | | |
| Total Shipping | | |
| **Total Enclosed** | | |

**Please Print**

Email

Name

Address

City _____ State _____ Zip _____

Phone _____ Country _____

Name on Card

Credit Card #

Expires

Signature

Prices subject to change without notice.Please allow 2-4 weeks for delivery

www.**QuiltedPhoto**.com